THE
GODDESS TAROT

٭ ٭ ٭

THE
GODDESS TAROT

Written and illustrated by

Kris Waldherr

↩ ↩ ↩

Publisher
U.S. Games Systems, Inc.
Stamford, CT 06902 USA

Other books by Kris Waldherr:

Embracing the Goddess Within:
A Creative Guide for Women

The Book of Goddesses

Persephone and the Pomegranate

↩ ↩ ↩

Library of Congress Cataloging-in-Publication Data

Waldherr, Kris.
    The Goddess Tarot/written and illustrated by Kris Waldherr.
        p.   cm.
    Includes bibliographical references.
    ISBN 1-57281-129-3 (pbk.)
    1. Tarot. 2. Goddesses. 3. Goddess religion. 4. Title.
BF1879.T2W32 1999
133.3'2424—dc21   98-43676
                                                  CIP

03 04 05 10 9 8 7 6 5

design by Kris Waldherr Art and Words
http://www.artandwords.com

©1999 U.S. GAMES SYSTEMS, INC.
PRINTED IN CANADA

U.S. GAMES SYSTEMS, INC.
Stamford, CT 06902 USA

TABLE OF CONTENTS

INTRODUCTION

The Goddess Tarot is a celebration of the Divine Feminine. Drawing inspiration from the many goddesses honored through history, The Goddess Tarot uses goddess myths and imagery to update traditional tarot symbolism; it acknowledges women's contemporary needs and mythic past. It is an easy-to-use, alternative deck for tarot readers already familiar with the popular Rider-Waite or Aquarian decks who seek a deeper experience of the Divine Feminine in their readings. For newcomers to the tarot, I hope the inclusion of goddess myths and symbolism will add relevance and depth.

Through my own personal experiences with tarot cards over the past fifteen years, I've come to think of the tarot as a potent archive of what I call "soul pictures"—pictures that reveal what Swiss psychiatrist C. G. Jung called the "collective unconscious," those subconscious rivers of mythic, archetypal experiences all humans possess within our psyches. To an observant eye, these soul pictures, through the use of symbols and images drawn from many cultures and spiritual traditions, possess layers of stories within stories. While the history of the tarot is unclear and mysterious, the stories told by these images still speak to our condition, addressing our common experiences as humans attempting to make sense of our lives and the world around us.

From the earliest times, humans have used stories and myths to understand the world around us and heal the soul. When we feel overwhelmed by life's sometimes confusing demands, these stories illustrate a larger view of life that is generous, wise, and accepting of the human condition.

As ancient and rich in stories and symbolism as the tarot may be, goddess myths are perhaps even more so—for these myths are *the* original women's stories. They show us the myriad ways women have been portrayed since ancient times. They reveal our collective feminine past, showing what cultures all around the world have revered, valued—and in some cases even feared—about women and our mysterious powers. These goddess stories speak to us through history's veils, telling us of women's innate divinity, dignity, and potency, showing the powers and talents all women possess: our abilities to create life from our bodies, our cycles of fertility that mirror the cycles of the moon, our strengths and beauties, our magic. They connect us to the celestial realm of the mystical as well as to the earthly realm of physical creation.

CREATING *THE GODDESS TAROT* ✧ ✧ ✧

Having been a tarot enthusiast for many years, I'd always dreamed of creating a deck of my own, one that would showcase women and their powers in a new light. Indeed, early in my professional career as an artist, I had created several pencil drawings of major arcana cards, but at that time felt too overwhelmed by the amount of work involved in a tarot deck to continue.

Years later, I was surprised to feel those old aspirations surface again. In a sense, the creation of *The Goddess Tarot* began with the research, writing, and painting of my book *The Book of Goddesses*.

It continued with the work on *The Book of Goddesses'* follow-up volume, *Embracing the Goddess Within: A Creative Guide for Women*. As I worked on these books, I noticed the stories and art I was creating mirrored in many ways the structure of the tarot's major arcana, from a Divinely Feminine perspective. I began to see how the art from *The Book of Goddesses* could lend itself to the creation of a tarot deck that could offer women a uniquely feminist way of examining their lives.

And so *The Goddess Tarot* began. While I worked on the deck, I felt strongly that I wanted to emphasize the values of creative agency and psychological understanding—in other words, personal empowerment—over any divinatory qualities usually associated with the tarot. It was also important to me that my deck be easily understood by those already comfortable with the symbolism of the Rider-Waite deck, which so many other decks use as their touchstone. As I proceeded onto the minor arcana, I looked to the Rider-Waite's imagery for inspiration but added a feminine twist: by recasting many of the figures of power within the minor arcana as women, I hope to have created a sense of psychological identification and empowerment for female tarot readers. For men who choose to work with *The Goddess Tarot*, who are interested in exploring their *anima*, or archetypal feminine side, I hope this rings true as well.

Ultimately, my intention in creating *The Goddess Tarot* was to create a tarot deck that would speak directly to women using *our* stories and archetypes, while incorporating the powerful symbolism of the tarot. Whether you are experiencing your first exposure to the tarot, are enthralled with goddesses, or an experienced tarot reader, I hope you will find *The Goddess Tarot* an essential instrument for your personal growth—as well as the reclamation of the Divine Feminine.

THE STRUCTURE OF *THE GODDESS TAROT* ⊹ ⊹ ⊹

Like most tarot decks, *The Goddess Tarot* contains seventy-eight cards. These seventy-eight cards are divided into 22 major arcana cards and 56 minor arcana cards. The word "arcana" is related to the word "arcane," meaning containing esoteric information—information available to those knowledgeable enough to understand the secret language of tarot symbolism. So that secret knowledge may become wisdom shared, each card and its imagery are explained in greater depth within this book.

In *The Goddess Tarot*, each major arcana card is related to a goddess and her story as well as a representation of an important aspect of life. Here is an overview of the major arcana:

NUMERAL	MAJOR ARCANA CARD	GODDESS
0	Beginnings	*Tara, Tibetan goddess of protection and compassion.*
I	Magic	*Isis, Egyptian fertility goddess.*
II	Wisdom	*Sarasvati, Hindu goddess of wisdom, education, and the arts.*
III	Fertility	*Estsanatlehi, Navajo goddess of the corn.*
IV	Power	*Freyja, Norse goddess of beauty and creativity.*
V	Tradition	*Juno, Roman ruling goddess.*
VI	Love	*Venus, Roman goddess of love.*
VII	Movement	*Rhiannon, Celtic horse goddess.*
VIII	Justice	*Athena, Greek goddess of wisdom.*

NUMERAL	MAJOR ARCANA CARD	GODDESS
IX	Contemplation	*Chang O, Chinese moon goddess.*
X	Fortune	*Lakshmi, Hindu goddess of fortune and prosperity.*
XI	Strength	*Oya, Yoruba goddess of the Niger River and the winds.*
XII	Sacrifice	*Kuan Yin, Chinese goddess of mercy.*
XIII	Transformation	*Ukemochi, Japanese food goddess.*
XIV	Balance	*Yemana, Santería goddess of the Caribbean Sea.*
XV	Temptation	*Nyai Loro Kidul, Javanese goddess of the waters.*
XVI	Oppression	*The Wawalak, sister Australian Aboriginal fertility goddesses.*
XVII	The Star	*Inanna, Sumerian goddess of the stars and heavens.*
XVIII	The Moon	*Diana, Roman goddess of the moon.*
XIX	The Sun	*The Zorya, a trio of Slavic guardian goddesses who attend the sun god.*
XX	Judgment	*Gwenhwyfar, Celtic sovereign goddess.*
XXI	The World	*Gaia, the Greek goddess who symbolizes the earth.*

The minor arcana of *The Goddess Tarot* is divided into four suits. Each suit is related to one of the four elements —earth, air, water, fire—as well as to a particular goddess and her myth.

Each suit features a different border depicting the colors and qualities of the element it is associated with. The suit of cups is associated with Venus, the Roman goddess of love; swords, Isis, the great Egyptian goddess who represents the journey of loss and redemption; pentacles, Lakshmi, the Hindu goddess of prosperity; and staves, Freyja, the Norse goddess of creativity and beauty. Here is an overview of the minor arcana:

SUIT	ELEMENT	QUALITY	GODDESS
CUPS	water, the moon	*receptive creativity, fertility, the Divine Feminine, personal relationships, family.*	Venus, the Roman goddess of love.
STAVES	fire, the sun	*active creativity, the masculine, inspiration, energy, communications, new ventures.*	Freyja, the Norse goddess of creativity and beauty.
SWORDS	air, salt	*intellect, discernment, cutting back for the sake of growth, introspection.*	Isis, the Egyptian fertility goddess.
PENTACLES	earth, gold	*material goods, business dealings, prosperity, fertility, results and completion.*	Lakshmi, the Hindu goddess of wealth, fortune and prosperity.

This book is set up in three parts, each one exploring a crucial area of *The Goddess Tarot*. Part One, The Major Arcana, explains each major arcana card and the goddess associated with it in greater depth. Part Two, The Minor Arcana, examines the energies, or paths, offered by every card in the four suits, including the goddess who represents each card. Finally, Part Three, Using The Goddess Tarot, gives the information necessary so you may use this original form of goddess wisdom.

As you work with *The Goddess Tarot*, I hope you find it to be a source of inspiration and empowerment that enables you to honor the divinity within yourself—and within all women throughout history.

Part One:

THE MAJOR ARCANA

M any consider the major arcana to tell a great story: the journey of humankind as they struggle to master various life lessons. In The Goddess Tarot, this story starts with the appropriately named card, Beginnings—affiliated with the Tibetan goddess Tara—and ends with the cumulative vision of The World, with twenty cards and goddesses in between.

Some consider the tarot to hold all the world's wisdom distilled into 78 potent images, as concentrated in symbolism as any dream. But, as with a dream, the meanings ascribed to these cards should be made pertinent to your life experiences; look upon these descriptions as a guide to spark your imagination and feelings.

Often when major arcana cards show up in tarot readings, they represent recurrent themes or important changes in a person's life, promising more to a situation than meets the eye. Also included are descriptions for reversed, or upside-down cards. These can be used according to your judgment; I personally prefer to think of cards as being strong or weak by taking into consideration the question being asked, their relative position in a spread (as explained in Part Three of this book), and the cards surrounding it.

0 – BEGINNINGS – Tara
Traditional card: The Fool
Keywords: New ventures, innocence, trust

The most important deity for Tibetan Buddhists is the compassionate mother goddess, Tara. Endowed with the power to heal all sorrows and grant all wishes, Tara often appears in many forms and colors, each one a different aspect of her divinity.

Tara is honored as the protectress against the many fears that block men and women from living in harmony. Stories about Tara reveal the kind of fears that concerned the people of ancient Tibet. She is reputed to protect her followers from the fear of elephants and poisonous snakes. But the most dangerous fears are often insidiously masked. These are also the ones that wreak the most damage—to our hopes, self-confidence, peace of mind—and keep us from meeting our full potential as human beings. Tara, whose sacred name translates as "she who causes one to cross," will help her devotees to cross safely to the other side of these fears to greater wisdom.

Meanings: Time for the start of a great journey. Innocence that allows one to be open to blessings. New beginnings. Optimism and trust. Feeling protected by divine forces.
Reversed or weakly aspected: A need to look deeper into an opportunity before proceeding. Folly or naiveity. Overconfidence—leaping before looking.

I – MAGIC – Isis

Traditional card: The Magician

Keywords: Self-empowerment, mastery

Associated with the Suit of Swords, page 123

The great Egyptian fertility goddess Isis is a potent symbol of the alchemic transformation this card suggests. For over 3000 years–from before 3000 B.C. to the second century A.D.–Isis was worshiped in Egypt as the Great Mother Goddess of the universe. She alone was the possessor of the secret name of Ra, the Egyptian ruling god, which gave her unlimited magical powers. Using these powers as well as the strength of her love, Isis was able to bring Osiris, her husband and brother, back to life for a short time after he was was murdered. Horus, the child she conceived of him during this time, grew to become one of the most powerful of the Egyptian gods.

Meanings: A growing awareness of the magic within yourself. A yearning to grow beyond perceived limitations. The ability to transform your life through the strength of originality and personal power. Renewed creativity and vigor. A new awareness of your power as you become in touch with your higher purpose. Experiencing the Divine Feminine as a power within yourself.

Reversed or weakly aspected: Blocked power, creativity. Manipulating others. A need to control situations from behind the scenes. Secrecy.

II – WISDOM – Sarasvati
Traditional card: The High Priestess
Keywords: Spirituality, education, enlightenment

Sarasvati, the Hindu goddess of knowledge and culture, is the divinely feminine embodiment of true wisdom, symbolizing spiritual knowledge as well as the refinement of the arts. Especially honored by scholars and musicians, Sarasvati is credited in India with creating the fruits of civilization: the first alphabet, the arts, mathematics, and music.

Extraordinarily beautiful and graceful, Sarasvati is easily recognizable by her dazzling white skin and brilliant clothing. Her brightness is said to represent the powerful, pure light of wisdom that destroys the danger of ignorance. Her four arms symbolize how her influence extends over the four directions of the earth and, by extension, all areas of life. The book she holds in one of her hands represents education. The beads she holds in another indicate spiritual knowledge. With her other hands she holds and plays the *vina*, an Indian lute, representing the art of music, which has the power to soothe with its beauty.

Meanings: An interest in spiritual knowledge. A teacher who will share with you what you are seeking—or perhaps you are that teacher. Wisdom gained in a graceful manner. Honoring the powers of intuition, dreams, the Divine Feminine.
Reversed or weakly aspected: Lack of trust in intuition. Over reliance on the intellect. Superficial knowledge. Fear of searching within oneself for answers.

III – FERTILITY – Estsanatlehi
Traditional card: The Empress
Keywords: Fecundity, abundance, growth

Perhaps better known as Changing Woman, this benevolent Navajo corn goddess symbolizes the ever-changing, ever-fertile earth. Like the earth itself, Estsanatlehi appears as a young maiden during the spring and summer months. As the wheel of the year changes to fall and winter, she also changes, taking on the features of an old crone.

Estsanatlehi is honored as the creator of the "Blessingway," a series of Navajo fertility rituals. The chants and ceremonies which make up the Blessingway are used for weddings, childbirth rites, and other happy occasions in the life of the Navajo. Each Blessingway takes place over several days. In addition to the many songs, rituals, and prayers that are part of this beautiful ceremony, pulverized flower blossoms, cornmeal, and pollen are spread upon the earth to fertilize it—and to incur the blessing of Estsanatlehi.

Meanings: Feelings of fertility and abundance. A new marriage or special relationship which celebrates one's growth as a woman. Creativity which manifests as physical product, whether that be children, artistic endeavors, or wealth. A pregnancy, either of yourself or someone close to you.

Reversed or weakly aspected: The opportunity to work through the manure of the past to better fertilize your life. Deprivation or sterility. Feeling the lack of material resources.

IV – POWER – Freyja
Traditional card: The Emperor
Keywords: Leadership, wisdom, authority

Associated with the Suit of Staves, page 93

Freyja, the Norse goddess of creativity, love, and beauty, expresses her power through her connection between the warring Aesir and the agriculturally peace-oriented Vanir—in this way she is a mediator between war and peace.

The Norse divided their gods and goddesses into two groups, the Vanir and the Aesir. Worshiped during the agricultural Bronze Age, the peaceful Vanir lived as one with the earth as they coaxed food from its fertile soil. Unfortunately the Iron Age brought not only the first development of hunting tools and weapons; it also brought with it the combative Aesir, who declared war upon the Vanir. For the sake of peace, the Vanir agreed to give the Aesir their beloved goddess of beauty, Freyja.

In this way, Freyja became the link between the old world—before iron tools—and the new, where power was often expressed in violence instead of through diplomacy and tolerance. She shows that true power lies in the ability to discriminate between aggression and passivity—and the ability to choose between them at the correct time.

Meanings: The ability to use power wisely. The awareness of one's power. Meeting an authority figure or teacher who can help. The ability to lead and inspire others. Knowledge of how to "work the system" without giving up important values or resorting to violence or deception.

Reversed or weakly aspected: Oppressed by another's power and authority. Insecurity. Loss of personal power. Passive aggression. Manipulating others.

V – TRADITION – Juno
Traditional card: The Hierophant
Keywords: Structure, conformity, ritual

The ancient Romans worshiped a powerful supreme goddess they called Juno. Honored as the patroness of marriage and other traditional rites of passages, the goddess was said to watch over and protect all women—from their first to last breath. For this reason Roman women called their souls "juno" in honor of the goddess.

Some of these traditional rites of passage are still practiced today, such as the marriage ceremony. To this day, many people consider the month of June, which still bears Juno's name, to be the most favorable time to marry. Another tradition which is no longer practiced is the Matronalia festival. Every year, on the first of March, the matrons of Rome traditionally held a special festival called the Matronalia to praise Juno and give thanks for her help. During this festival, they asked the goddess to bless their marriages and help them give birth to healthy babies.

Meanings: Following established social structures and traditions. In love relationships, the desire for marriage, declaration of intentions for the sake of security. Awareness of public image and the desire to control it. Wanting to conform in order to gain society's or an authority figure's approval. Possible rigidity.

Reversed or weakly aspected: The need to throw out old social structures which may no longer be fulfilling your needs. Fear of unconventional ideas and ways of approach. Nonconformity. Questioning traditions.

VI – LOVE – Venus

Traditional card: The Lovers

Keywords: Harmony, passion, sexuality

Associated with the Suit of Cups, page 63

Venus, the Roman goddess of love, brings joy to gods and humans as well as to the plant world. Accordingly, she is associated with the arrival of spring, that most love-inspiring of seasons. Created from the happy union of sea and sky, Venus has been described by many as "the queen of pleasure." It is Venus who inspires people to love each other and to enjoy the pleasures of sensuality and passion. However, with these delights comes responsibility for another's happiness; the more one loves, the more open the lover is to the beloved, the more hearts entwine to become one.

Meanings: A renewed awareness of the nature of passionate love—and what is needed to encourage it. Artistic creativity. Sexuality. The integration within oneself of the masculine and feminine, the god and the goddess—the Divine Marriage, if you will. A new, important relationship. Self-esteem.

Reversed or weakly aspected: Manipulating others with sexuality. Inability to find a loving partner. Immaturity and irresponsibility in love relationships. Game playing. Disharmony.

VII – MOVEMENT – Rhiannon
Traditional card: The Chariot
Keywords: Timing, transition, change

The British horse goddess Rhiannon is said to appear to her
followers riding an unearthly white horse. In this way, Rhiannon
symbolizes the unceasing force of movement that pulls all of life
along with it. Dressed in royal robes of gold, Rhiannon is always
accompanied by three magical birds from the Happy Otherworld,

where gods and goddesses live. The ethereal song of these birds was believed to have the power to lull the living to death, restore the dead to life, and heal all sorrow.

Rhiannon's name is derived from "rigantona," which means "great queen goddess." In an earlier period, she was known as Epona. Many statues of her as Epona have been found, most of them depicting her with a mare on one side and a bundle of grain on the other. This image best symbolizes movement's eventual end: the great cumulation of harvest.

Meanings: Movement into the next phase of life. If you are feeling impatient, don't worry–transitions will go smoothly, as if you are being pulled by the twin forces of fate and fortune. External forces that work with you. Career advancement. Good timing!

Reversed or weakly aspected: Necessity of waiting. Impatience. Inconvenient timing. Disregard or insensitivity to the signs around yourself. Feeling trapped or unable to make a transition.

VIII – JUSTICE – Athena
Traditional card: Justice
Keywords: Wisdom, fairness, detachment

Athena, the Greek goddess of wisdom, was one of the most powerful of the ancient Greek goddesses. Often depicted with an owl as a
symbol of enlightenment, and a serpent as a symbol of fertility,
Athena's brilliance of reason was said to be as penetrating as her
clear, gray eyes. She was the daughter of Zeus, the Greek father

god, and his first wife, Metis, whose name meant "wisdom." Though her beauty brought her attention from many, she chose to remain unattached, preferring the land of the intellect over the ocean of romantic entanglements.

In time, Athena came to be revered, not only as the goddess of wisdom, but also as the goddess of war. Though Athena was skilled without equal in the art of battle, she valued peace over discord and gave her protection to only those in need of defense.

Meanings: The need for a more detached viewpoint towards a troublesome situation. Imagine you are as wise as Athena and look at the situation. What should you do? Are you being fair to yourself and those around you? Worry not—you will be able to defend yourself; reasonable ears will hear and justice will be done.

Reversed or weakly aspected: Frustration with bureaucracies or organizations. Impatience with red tape. The appearance of this card shows that this is a temporary situation.

IX – CONTEMPLATION – Chang O
Traditional card: The Hermit
Keywords: Meditation, withdrawal, introspection

Chang O, the Chinese moon goddess, symbolizes the need for withdrawal from the world in order to contemplate the universal questions of life.

Before Chang O became a moon goddess, she lived among the other gods and goddesses with her husband, Yi, the Divine Archer.

But when Yi shot nine suns out of the sky, leaving only one to warm the earth, the unlucky couple were stripped of their immortality and forced to live among humans. Chang O was dismayed and begged her husband to seek the potion of immortality from the goddess Hsi Wang Mu. Hsi Wang Mu was sympathetic, so she gave Yi enough for them to become immortal—but not enough for them to become god and goddess again. But Chang O had an idea. If she drank Yi's portion as well as her own, perhaps she would become a goddess again. After all, she reasoned, she was not the one who shot down the suns, so why should she be punished? Too tempted to resist, she drank it all. Soon, Chang O felt herself become as light as ether as she floated away toward the heavens. Before she knew it, she was on the moon, once again a beautiful goddess—but unable to leave because of her weightlessness. There she spent eternity alone contemplating the separation between humanity and divinity.

Meanings: The need to go within, to gain knowledge to one's own divinity. Withdrawal to better contemplate life's direction. Retreat into inner life—at this time, your needs are not so focused on relationships with others, but on your relationship with yourself.

Reversed or weakly aspected: Distracting oneself by immersion in the world. Refusal to listen to intuition. No time to think or reflect. Superficiality.

X – FORTUNE – Lakshmi
Traditional card: The Wheel of Fortune
Keywords: Prosperity, expansion, chance

Associated with the Suit of Pentacles, page 153

The Hindu goddess of good fortune and prosperity, Lakshmi is believed to be attracted to sparkling jewels—which are like the riches she bestows upon worshippers who have pleased her. To woo her favor, every November, on the night of the new moon, Indian women clean their homes and hang tiny lanterns that glitter like diamonds in the darkness. Not surprisingly, many believe she lives in the sky with the stars, whose gem-like brilliance adorns her beauty.

In Hindu mythology, Lakshmi is believed to represent all that is feminine, while her consort, Vishnu, known as the Conqueror of Darkness, represents all that is masculine. Paintings from India often show Lakshmi and Vishnu riding on the back of Garuda, the giant king of birds, as they fly across the land spreading fortune.

Meanings: The generosity of the universe. The ability to be open to abundance. Feelings of expansion and positive expectations. Awareness of beauty and love. Chance.

Reversed or weakly aspected: Uncomfortable feelings or experiences with chance. Disappointment. Unexpected endings or beginnings. Capriciousness.

XI – STRENGTH – O_{ya}
Traditional card: Strength
Keywords: Courage, inner strength, leadership

The storm gales that Oya, the Nigerian goddess of the wind, creates are strong enough to tear the roofs off houses and uproot
huge trees. Since words are made of the wind we exhale when we
breathe—and since Oya is praised for her eloquent speech—
women often ask her for the right words to ease conflicts and gain

power. Because of this, Oya is considered a powerful patroness of female strength and leadership.

To please Oya, many Yoruba wear strings of maroon beads around their necks. They keep altars in their homes displaying objects sacred to her: buffalo or "bush cow" horns, a copper crown symbolizing the copper palace where she lives, and her favorite bean cakes. Oya is still widely worshiped among the Yoruba.

Meanings: Any strength and any wisdom you need are within you now. Powers of speech to transform weakness into strength. Integrity and adherence to one's vision. The strength to create peace between opposing forces. These forces may be internalized or personified in a situation. Tame them—you have the strength!
Reversed or weakly aspected: The scattering of energies. Imbalance. Creating discord for the sake of sport. Valuing the lower energies over the higher.

XII – SACRIFICE – Kuan Yin
Traditional card: The Hanged Man
Keywords: Compassion, surrender, patience

Honored as the holy mother of compassion and mercy, Kuan Yin is one of the most beloved goddesses of China. After her death, Kuan Yin was brought to heaven, where her purity of heart and mercy toward others transformed her into a goddess. Instead of allowing herself to enjoy heaven's delights, out of pity for humanity's suffering the goddess begged to be sent back to earth to help anyone in need—vowing never to leave until sorrow was vanquished forever.

Kuan Yin sacrificed herself for the greater good of all. Because she personifies boundless compassion and loving kindness, devotees of Kuan Yin believe that even the act of speaking her name bring reliefs from pain. Some say that she walks among us still, looking after the many in need of her care.

Meanings: A surrender to higher principles, higher goals. Self-abnegation. The ability to take care of others in a compassionate, nurturing way. Sacrifice in order to make sacred, to gain enlightenment. Empathy.

Reversed or weakly aspected: Avoiding pain for gain. Lack of compassion. Focus on materialism to the determent of spiritualty. Displacing fears unto others.

XIII –TRANSFORMATION– Ukemochi
Traditional card: Death
Keywords: Endings and beginnings, change

After her death, the body of the Japanese food goddess Ukemochi was transformed to supply food and other goods to nurture all of humanity. Her head turned into cows, who ran off to populate the earth, and grain sprouted from her forehead. Then rice plants sprouted from her belly, their seed scattering everywhere and sprouting into new plants. Finally, her inky eyebrows twisted into silkworms, whose threads wove into rainbow-colored silks that clothed the gods and goddesses, protecting them from the harsh elements.

And so, through Ukemochi's transcending power, life was transformed from death—starting a new cycle of continuance.

Meanings: Transformations. The need to allow something to die in order to create room for the new. Change which may feel painful at first, but is necessary. Creating life out of death, in order to nurture oneself or others.

Reversed or weakly aspected: Stagnation and fear of change. Resisting transformations. Adherence to the status quo. The need to move in a new direction, but the inability to do so. Rigidity. Displacing fears onto others.

XIV–BALANCE–Yemana

Traditional card: Temperance

Keywords: Harmony, self-control, balance

Yemana, a beautiful and powerful Santeria goddess of the ocean, is the daughter of the earth goddess Odduddua, and the sister-wife of the god Aganju. As the divine mother of the fourteen gods and goddesses who make up the sacred pantheon, she occupies an exalted position in the Santeria religion. The goddess of water,

Yemana is often called upon to provide rain, water that nurtures all of life. This water from the heavens represents the necessary balance between heaven and earth, creativity and depletion—a balance which brings harmony to all who experience it.

Followers of Yemana often call her by the honorific "Holy Queen Sea." Not surprisingly, she is believed to own all the riches of the ocean: seashells, pearls, oysters, coral reefs, and every creature within its fertile depths.

Meanings: Experiencing—or seeking—a deep sense of harmony and union. Integration. Moderation. Balance between the spiritual (symbolized by water) and the physical (symbolized by earth). Integration and moderation. Union of the conscious and unconscious forces of life.

Reversed or weakly aspected: Imbalance. Discomfort. Inability to find peace within or with others. Lack of moderation.

XV –TEMPTATION– Nyai Loro Kidul
Traditional card: The Devil
Keywords: Inner turmoil, illusion, obsession

Below the deep green waves of the Pacific Ocean that surround Java resides the seductive goddess, Nyai Loro Kidul. Many know better than to swim in the waters where the goddess rules; it is believed that she looks there for mortals to serve her in her undersea realm. Nyai Loro Kidul's elusive powers reflect the temptations of illusion, of beauties which enslave rather than enrich, of uncontrollable desires and passions.

The Javanese still honor Nyai Loro Kidul today. A seductive mermaid queen, she symbolizes the mysterious hidden forces of the ocean—forces whose powers must be respected. To appease the goddess, people leave offerings of coconuts, clothes, and even fingernail clippings by the ocean's edge—all of which are eagerly accepted by the swirling sea.

Meanings: Tempted by forces one cannot control, like undercurrents from the ocean. Something deep and dark within the psyche—what Jung termed the shadow—is personified as temptation or addiction. Sensual desires. Gluttony or envy. Experiencing the envy of others. Feelings of lack of control. The need to be controlling.

Reversed or weakly aspected: Freedom from temptation. Mastery over something previously controlling—a habit, a person, or a wound from the past. Transforming a weakness into a strength. The acceptance of one's darker, or shadow side.

XVI – OPPRESSION – The Wawalak
Traditional card: The Tower
Keywords: Confusion, difficulties, release

During the Dreamtime, a mythic time when gods and goddess still walked the earth, the Wawalak, a pair of Australian aboriginal sister goddesses, accidentally polluted the sacred waterhole of Yurlungur, the Great Rainbow Serpent, with a single drop of menstrual blood. In angry response, rains poured down and the waterhole flooded. The two sisters sang and sang, hoping to appease the serpent as well as to protect their newborn babies. But Yurlungur emerged from the waterhole and swallowed the sisters, along with their infants, in a huge gulp.

Oppressed by darkness, fear, and guilt, the Wawalak wept within the deepest belly of the serpent—until they were reborn from Yurlungur's mouth back into the light. As both goddesses and mothers, the Wawalak symbolize the unending force of life in all women, a force that can never be oppressed for long.

Meanings: Feeling overwhelmed or oppressed by circumstances or emotions. Depression. Like the Wawalak, the "light" has left your life; you are waiting to be released from the darkness. A new start after a painful ending that may have shattered your view of the world. A pause before moving into a new phase of life.

Reversed or weakly aspected: Though your situation may feel overwhelming and intimidating, hidden forces are at work to transform things for the better. Be patient and trusting.

XVII–THE STAR–Inanna
Traditional card: The Star
Keywords: Inspiration, hope, dreams

Inanna, the great goddess of the Bronze Age, was honored with the title "Queen of Heaven." She was said to be clothed with the stars, wearing the zodiac itself wrapped around her waist as an ornate light-studded girdle. In Sumeria, where she was worshiped five thousand years ago, Inanna's temple was called "Eanna," which means "house of heaven." Even today we look to Inanna's heavenly stars for our dreams and aspirations.

Besides ruling over the heavens, Inanna was credited with power over the most important aspects of Sumerian life. Because they believed that all moisture was caused by the moon, Inanna was also the goddess of the rain clouds, which provided water needed for the grain to grow.

Meanings: Awareness of goals and dreams, and the self-respect and strength to follow them. Success, good fortune, creativity. There are great possibilities of success with the appearance of this card. All is well with the world; your highest hopes are supported by the universe. Any feelings of insecurity and unworthiness are to be banished from your thoughts. Follow your dreams without fear or censure—don't be afraid to work to make them happen! *Reversed or weakly aspected:* Not following your bliss. Insecurity. Feelings of unworthiness. Not listening to intuition. Fear of following your dreams or reaching a goal.

XVIII – THE MOON – Diana
Traditional card: The Moon
Keywords: Femininity, intuition, emotion

In ancient Rome, Diana was honored as the goddess of wild animals, hunting, and the moon. The changing moon reflects the cycles of nature; its light influences all growing things—plants, animals, and humans alike—for better and for worse. Diana reminds us of our connection to these cycles and that, like the moon itself, what is empty will, in time, become full if we are patient.

Worship of Diana extended across Europe from Rome, and she was still believed to rule the wild forests until the Middle Ages. Then, many people forgot that she was a goddess; they called her queen of the witches instead. They had forgotten that Diana symbolized the Divine Feminine's ability to provide nurturing for all of its creatures, great and small.

Meanings: The receptive, nurturing aspects of the Divine Feminine. Intense emotions. Vivid or lucid dreams. Intuition. An opportunity to work on your relationship with that which truly nurtures you. The support of caring women.

Reversed or weakly aspected: Discomforted by emotional situations. Uneasiness with intuition, maternal figures, women. Feeling as changeable as the moon—instead of seeing this as a negative, recognize that what is empty will become full again in time.

XIX – THE SUN – The Zorya
Traditional card: The Sun
Keywords: Creativity, success, fertility

In Slavic mythology, the Zorya are a trinity of sister goddesses who attend to the sun god, whose chariot rides through the sky every day, bringing light and warmth. The sun represents the brilliance of the life force—the incisiveness of intellect, the inspiration of creativity, the light that nourishes all life, plant and human.

As well as attending to the sun god, without whose light all living things would perish, the Zorya are believed to be the guardians of the universe. As such, they stand watch over a fierce doomsday hound subdued by only a chained leash—legend says that if ever this chain were to break, the end of the world would be at hand.

Meanings: An expansive, life-affirming energy. Creativity and inspiration. Relationships with children. Procreation. Love and sexuality. Masculine, or yang, energy.

Reversed or weakly aspected: Unwillingness to accept affection. Problems with children. Creativity blocked by external or internal forces. Delays in expanding unto the next phase of a project. Feeling thwarted.

XX – JUDGMENT – Gwenhwyfar
Traditional card: Judgment
Keywords: Sovereignty, confidence, decisions

Gwenhwyfar, the Welsh goddess and first lady of the islands and sea, is believed to have existed as long as there was surf to pound against rocky shore. Praised for her judgment and wisdom, it was prophesied that no man could rule Wales without her by his side— it is little wonder that many would-be kings attempted to abduct the once and future queen, since they foolishly thought that to possess her would make them king. They did not understand that it was Gwenhwyfar's judgment which made them sovereign, rather than any romantic entanglement.

Meanings: Important decisions or news. Movement into the next phase of life. Time for a major and necessary change in life—often welcome, but frightening because of its magnitude. The confidence of a queen.

Reversed or weakly aspected: Stagnation. Inability to act. Blockage. Giving up authority rather than living up to one's potential.

XXI – THE WORLD – Gaia
Traditional card: The World
Keywords: Interconnection, expansion, travel

For thousands of years and in cultures all around the globe, the Great Goddess was worshiped in one form or another. In ancient Greece, the earth was personified as Gaia, a goddess who existed before all other life and created all of life. At her shrine at Delphi, Gaia was honored by priestesses who threw sacred herbs into a cauldron, using the fragrant smoke to invoke the goddess' eternal wisdom.

The story of Gaia reminds us of the interconnection of all of life—and the importance of living in harmony with her resources, as well as among our fellow humans. To experience this harmony within ourselves, as well as in the world, is perhaps the greatest gift of all.

Meanings: The Divine Feminine in action. Experiencing connection with the universe, the source which nurtures us all. A sense of expansion and hope. Travel and communications. Career expansions. Hope. An awareness of the fragile ecological balance we are all responsible for as residents of earth.

Reversed or weakly aspected: Fear of expansion. Feeling pessimistic about the future; even if you're uncertain how it will manifest, you *are* moving into a more hopeful period of life. Trust!

Part Two:
THE MINOR ARCANA

Four suits, each associated with a particular goddess, make up the minor arcana of The Goddess Tarot. Each suit is an invitation to follow the path of wisdom that each goddess embodies. Cups promise the emotional satisfaction of Venus, the Roman goddess of love. Staves offer the talent and initiative of Freyja, the Norse goddess of creativity. Swords tell of the understanding of Isis, gained through difficulties transformed into wisdom. The physical beauty and wealth of pentacles are offered to those who follow the path that Lakshmi, the Hindu goddess of fortune, symbolizes.

Each numbered card in the minor arcana shows a woman as she undergoes the journey represented by each suit. She is meant to represent "everywoman"—perhaps the querant herself—as an aspect of the goddess and her suit: just as we embody the Goddess, the Goddess embodies all of us. Each number symbolizes a different stage of growth in the development of the suit—beginning with one, the purist expression, and cumulating in ten. Court cards (here represented as prince, princess, king, and queen) can reveal different views of the same woman's psyche at different times of life: masculine, feminine, young, old, innocent, wise. On a more mundane level, court cards can also represent people or situations surrounding the querant.

When minor arcana cards appear in a reading, think of them as filling in the particulars of a situation—the people involved, the emotions, the everyday unfolding of events—as opposed to the sweeping changes often shown by the major arcana. For it is here in the minor arcana that the sacred issues explored by the major arcana are made human.

THE SUIT OF CUPS
The Path of Venus

Element: Water, the moon

Corresponds to Love, major arcana card number 6

The suit of cups is associated with Venus, the Roman goddess of love and beauty. Cups symbolize the receptive aspect of the Divine Feminine—think of the Holy Grail whose mystical contents nurture spirit and flesh; think of a woman's womb whose fertile waters bring new life from the void. It is from the suit of cups that everything begins. Without the ability to be receptive to inspiration nothing can come into being—relationships, creative projects, or spiritual enlightenment.

The cups proffered by Venus are an invitation to us to drink deeply of the magical water of love, life, inspiration, and pleasure. They offer us our first experience of the Divine Feminine at her purest and most potent.

THE MYTH OF VENUS ✤ ✤ ✤

Conceived and born of fertile sea, Venus is the bringer of joy to humans as well as to the plant world. For it is love that begins the cycle of creation by inspiring us with noble thoughts of beauty and love. For this reason, artists and poets have turned to Venus for hundreds of years for help with their artistic endeavors and humans have beseeched Venus to favor their romances. Often described as "the queen of pleasure," Venus is associated with the arrival of spring, that most love-inducing of seasons.

Perhaps because she craved passion and love as much as she inspired it, Venus' romantic life was as complicated as some of the ones she blessed. While married to Vulcan, the lame god of the forge, she was also involved with Mars, the god of war. But it was with a mortal man, Anchises, that she gave birth to Aeneas, the hero of *The Aeneid*. Aeneas was a Trojan prince who escaped after the fall of Troy and sailed to Italy, where he founded the Roman Empire; and so through her son, Venus came to be considered the mother of the Roman people.

ACE OF CUPS

Keywords: The Divine Feminine, love, creativity

Here the full moon is contained—but not captured—within a golden cup surrounded by the ocean, source of all life. Engraved upon this ornate goblet are ancient symbols of the Divine Feminine. Among these are the ancient triangle known as the *delphos*, whose womb-like shape celebrates the great trinity of earth, sea, and sky as well as the three stages of women; within the *delphos* is the glyph for Venus, the Roman goddess of love, who was born of sea. The gentle light from the moon illuminates our most deeply held yearnings for pleasure, love, and emotional satisfaction. Water overflows from the cup, suggesting the richness of our emotions: they are so full of hope that they are literally spilling over in anticipation and celebration.

Meanings: The Divine Feminine. The beginning of a new cycle ripe with potential and happiness. Great happiness. Start of a new love or friendship that will be important and emotionally nurturing. Creative inspiration and receptivity—a visitation from the Muses. *Reversed or weakly aspected:* Emotional disappointment. Creative blockages. Disillusionment with love. Sadness or melancholy. Too much internalizing.

TWO OF CUPS

Keywords: Harmony, partnership, love

In a mysterious moonlit garden, the woman and her beloved pledge their faith. The woman, dressed in veils and robes of white, looks like the moon come down to earth. Inspired and made beautiful by love, she embodies the Divine Feminine to her lover; she is as enchanting as Venus, whose beauty inspires men and women to thoughts of harmony, love, and pleasure. Her lover, intoxicated by the possibilities that this woman represents, is healed and made whole by honoring her as his equal and opposite. Together they celebrate the divine marriage of the feminine to the masculine.

Meanings: Harmony. Love. Enchantment. Integration of masculine and feminine aspects within oneself. An attraction that may become an important friendship or love relationship.

Reversed or weakly aspected: Infatuation. Disillusionment within a love relationship or close friendship. Overindulging in sensuality for the sake of the "high."

THREE OF CUPS

Keywords: Celebration, joy, harmony

The woman dances with two other women in a circle, one older than her, the other younger. The wine intoxicates them, bringing warmth to their emotions and inspiration to their souls. Together they symbolize the three stages of woman—maid, mother, crone—that comprise the circle of life. The crone in the fullness of life, raises her cup of knowledge and shares her wisdom with the woman. The youngest woman, the maiden, invigorates her with her youthful energy and new ideas. The woman, the mother, centered between the two in the middle of her life's journey, feels pleasure and harmony as they dance; she is filled with satisfaction. Together, these dancing women symbolize all of life's joys, potentials, and riches—all sacred to the goddess Venus.

Meanings: Great satisfaction. A reason to celebrate. Peace between family generations. A celebration involving women. Possibly a wedding feast.

Reversed or weakly aspected: Overindulgence. Procrastination. Distracting oneself with pleasure. Too much partying—time to get to work!

FOUR OF CUPS

Keywords: Dissatisfaction, overindulgence, boredom

After overindulging in pleasures, the woman sits beneath a tree with her eyes closed, hoping to ground herself after the excitement of intoxication. Behind her is the sea, symbolizing emotions, and a distant landscape; all that she no longer feels connected to. Four cups rest before her still offering their magical water—

but she has drunk too much; it no longer has any value for her. A waning sickle moon mirrors the emptiness she is feeling.

Meanings: Too much of a good thing. Taking something for granted—love, talents, beauty. Discontent. Need for re-evaluation of a relationship. Narcissism.

Reversed or weakly aspected: Acceptance of the situation, though discontent is still present. A passing phase.

FIVE OF CUPS

Keywords: Disappointment, sadness, pessimism

Night has fallen upon a desolate landscape decorated with five golden cups. Three of these cups have tipped over, spilling their magical water upon arid rocks. Disappointed, the woman, dressed in dark robes of mourning, leaves them behind to search for something better. Even though a few stars twinkle with hope at the horizon, the moonless night is so dark that the woman cannot see them. Nor can she see the promise of Venus offered by the two cups still upright—despite her pessimism, all is not lost.

Meanings: Disappointment or disillusionment with intimate relationships. Concentrating on problems instead of assets. Desire to move on. Creative blockage or infertility. Pessimism or depression. *Reversed or weakly aspected:* A growing awareness that relationships are what you make of them. The ability to drink of the two remaining cups, which symbolize the promise of attraction and love.

SIX OF CUPS

Keywords: Memories, nostalgia, children

In a dream, the woman sees the tide rise around six generously proportioned cups. Pulled by the moon's gravity, salt water floods around three cups. The remaining three rest upon an entry way to a thatched cottage full of memories and hopes of the past. These cups are filled with wisteria as a sacred offering to Venus, who brings forth flowers from the earth—symbolizing the rejuvenative aspects of the Divine Feminine.

Meanings: Harmonious home. Nostalgia. Children and childhood memories. Longing for the sweetness of the past, and its innocence. The ability to create sweetness within the home, incorporating the strengths of the past into the present.

Reversed or weakly aspected: Need to examine the past, including perhaps painful memories. The key to understanding may be locked there.

SEVEN OF CUPS

Keywords: Choices, indecisiveness, fantasy

Surrounded by seven gold cups, the woman tries to choose but is
unable. The cups contain symbols of different futures: the rose
symbolizing the pleasures of Venus; the jeweled crown of earthly
success; the laurels of victory; a castle; the snake of rejuvenation;
and finally, a skull representing death and the afterlife. A cloth
covers the mysterious contents of the seventh cup—it contains

the unknown. Surrounded by so many possibilities, the woman's eyes are closed, suggesting the need to look within—or the need to wake up from fantastic dreams.

Meanings: Overindulging in thoughts of what the future may bring. Daydreams. A choice is needed, a decision made in order to move forward and rejoin the world.

Reversed or weakly aspected: Allowing fantasies to influence how you view life—time to be more realistic. Projecting onto others instead of seeing things as they truly are.

EIGHT OF CUPS

Keywords: Leavetakings, disillusionment

In an empty, almost lunar-like landscape, the tide has retreated;
a waning moon is just a sliver of light in a dark starless night.
Within this mysterious setting, the woman walks away from eight
cups that she has drunken of. She is searching for more substantial
fare to feed her spirit. Though she knows the eight cups are empty,
she looks back nonetheless, questioning her actions, hoping her

decision to move on is correct. She wonders if she will ever again feel the pleasure and love represented by the goddess Venus.

Meanings: Time to move on. Need for more substance in life—whether that be more satisfying relationships, a more authentic way of life. Leavetakings.

Reversed or weakly aspected: Lingering too long in a difficult or superficial situation. Uncertainty about a relationship, whether to stay or leave. Doubts.

NINE OF CUPS

Keywords: The granting of wishes, sensuality

Finally, satisfaction! A rainbow leads the woman to a banquet table set with nine cups filled with delicious, rare wines. Surrounded by soft green grass and delicate pink flowers—pink being the sacred color of Venus—this table is covered with a rich blue cloth embroidered with golden moons; these decorations symbolizing the emotional riches offered by the Divine Feminine. Well worth waiting for, this sumptuous feast will nourish many bodies and souls. As the woman rests in this garden of earthly delights, she raises her cup in thanks.

Meanings: Great satisfaction. Contentment. Some consider this card the "wish" card—meaning a wish will be granted if this card appears in a spread. Earthly delights.

Reversed or weakly aspected: Delay in the granting of your wishes. Complacency. Taking a relationship for granted. Overindulgence. Inability to receive pleasure.

TEN OF CUPS

Keywords: Joyful closure, abundance, happiness

As the woman gazes from her celebratory feast, she sees a rainbow crowning a serene sky. Ten cups form a golden arc over it. They are reflected in a calm ocean—the same ocean from which the goddess Venus was born, bringing love and harmony to all who would know these joys. The moon, symbolizing the Divine Feminine and the robust bounties she offers, is full and promises satisfaction, abundance, and love. As the woman gazes upon this beauteous scene, she decides that this is the best life can offer.

Meanings: Joyful completion. Happy family life. Abundance. Great emotional satisfaction. Endurance in love relationships. Happiness and joy. Fertility and expansion.

Reversed or weakly aspected: An inability to allow joy to be experienced. Dissatisfaction, though uncertain why—everything looks perfect on the surface.

PRINCE OF CUPS

Keywords: Gentleness, intuition, an invitation

Surrounded by a calm ocean, the Prince of Cups, a gentle boy about
to blossom into young adulthood, proffers a cup. It is decorated
with the sacred symbols of Venus and the Divine Feminine, for
whom he is a representative. The water within this cup is a magical potion—it can invite love, renewed passion, creative ventures,
or intuition for the recipient. The darkened night sky and calm

waters surrounding the Prince of Cups suggests a quiet acceptance of his offer.

Meanings: An invitation or offer. Gentleness. Children whose open hearts allow one to experience innocence anew. Intuition. Prophetic or inspiring dreams.

Reversed or weakly aspected: Disillusionment with an offer that promised more substance. Fickleness or immaturity of affection. Inconsistent or unreliable messages. Ambivalence.

PRINCESS OF CUPS

Keywords: Inspiration, grace, pleasure

The Princess of Cups, an adolescent girl as beautiful as Venus, is crowned with gold and a brilliant waxing moon. The sheer force of her allure attracts artistry, inspiration, and new opportunities. Anticipating love, pleasure, and the ripeness of womanhood, she drinks fully of the cup's refreshing contents. As she drinks, she closes her eyes to take in the fullness of her spirit, soul, and serenity—all that she offers to those who experience her graceful presence.

Meanings: Artistic inspiration and receptivity. Movement in these areas of life. Grace and talent. A young woman who symbolizes the gifts of Venus—love, beauty, and emotional richness—and inspires others to appreciation.

Reversed or weakly aspected: The need to be more receptive to beauty, love, and harmony. Overindulgence in fantasies.

KING OF CUPS

Keywords: Practical artistry, mastery

The King of Cups, a thoughtful older man who is quiet and serene in nature, sits upon his throne. He is surrounded by water, symbolizing his authority over the world of emotions and intuition. As he meditates upon the single cup held within his palm, he is entranced by the potential promised to him by the Divine Feminine. Masterful and artistic, the King of Cups is able to express himself in his relationships and work; he is a consort worthy of any follower of the goddess Venus.

Meanings: Ability to live up to ideals and dreams. Combining artistic integrity with the needs of the marketplace. Emotional maturity and integrity. Someone who symbolizes these forces.

Reversed or weakly aspected: Desire to have more control over one's artistic aspirations. Need to stop dreaming up schemes and get to work. Inconsistency.

QUEEN OF CUPS

Keywords: Soulfulness, emotion, inspiration

The full moon is a halo silhouetting the heavy golden crown of the majestic Queen of Cups. Holding all wisdom and intuition within herself, she is more soul than body. A profusion of pearls dot her gown and headdress, these jewels from the sea symbolizing the fertile emotional forces of the Divine Feminine. Like the sea herself, the Queen of Cups' regal mysterious presence inspires people to look within. She knows the treasures found there will nourish the heart and lead to greater happiness.

Meanings: Mastery of all that Venus—and the suit of cups—represents: art, beauty, intimacy, love. The ability to express love, to nurture others. An older woman who inspires others to live harmoniously.

Reversed or weakly aspected: Overwhelmed by emotions that need sorting. Need to take control of these feelings. Not mining the treasures of the soul. Disharmonious relationships with women—or with the self.

THE SUIT OF STAVES
The Path of Freyja

Element: Fire, the sun

Corresponds to Power, major arcana card number 4

The suit of staves is related to Freyja, the Norse goddess of creativity, fertility, and beauty. In the progression of the minor arcana's suits, staves are like new tree saplings breaking through the earth—fertile earth that has been anointed with water from the preceding suit of cups.

Staves are the active aspect of the Divine Feminine. Like conduits of the sun's procreative force, they channel energy to areas and encourage growth. Staves bring exciting movement to a tarot reading, much like the movement displayed by Freyja as she rides through the sky in her chariot drawn by magical grey cats.

THE MYTH OF FREYJA ✧ ✧ ✧

In Norse mythology, gods and goddesses are divided into two groups, the Vanir and the Aesir. The peaceful Vanir grew food from the earth and were worshiped during the agricultural Bronze Age. Later, when the first tools and weapons were developed with forge and fire, the combative Aesir came into existence. The Aesir brought war and discord into the bucolic world of the Vanir. Desiring peace at any price, the Vanir offered the Aesir their most precious daughter: Freyja, daughter of Njord, the god of fair winds.

In this way, Freyja became a mediator between peace and violence. A goddess of creativity, sexuality, and beauty, she also became known as the goddess who presided over the living and the dead; for it was Freyja who was responsible for the souls of half of the warriors felled in battle. Upon their death, these men were brought to Freyja's grand hall in Asgard, where they were feted with epic poems of brave deeds and accorded honor.

Appropriately, sacred to Freyja were the pragmatic arts of goldsmithing and jewelry making—crafts which take the raw materials of the earth and turn them into beautiful treasures.

ACE OF STAVES

Keywords: Inspiration, growth, action

Upon a verdant green hill dotted with tiny red flowers, a single
sapling grows, stretching toward the sky like Freyja in her magical
chariot drawn by grey cats. New leaves twist from its knotty stub-
born surface, revealing the vigorous growth surging within its
woody depths. Behind this single stave, the fiery sun—symbolizing
the Divine Feminine's dynamic life force that inspires us to grow,

prosper, and understand—rises upon a distant mountain range. It is the start of a new day with new possibilities for action as well as new opportunities for growth.

Meaning: The active principle of the Divine Feminine. Great energy that flows unbounded. Beginning of a focused, creative period. Inspiration that inspires action. New opportunities. The active, or yang, aspect of life. Growth.

Reversed or weakly aspected: Difficulties with new ventures. Being "burned" out by too much energy, too much expenditure, too many thoughts. The need to focus.

TWO OF STAVES

Keywords: New ventures, partnership, ideas

Inspired by new ideas, the woman watches the sun rise, and plans how to bring her vision into the world. A stave stands on each side of her. The stave she holds in her left hand symbolizes her receptivity to new ideas; the other stave represents her aspirations in the world beyond her. She is dressed in a red gown—the color of vigor and beginnings—as she surveys the mountain range within sight from her ornately walled terrace. She has the confidence and talent of Freyja, the goddess of creativity; this ensures she will meet success.

Meanings: Beginnings of a new venture, possibly business-oriented in nature. A dynamic partnership. New ideas that transform lives and energize people. Transforming inspiration into action.

Reversed or weakly aspected: A good start to a venture that eventually loses momentum. Disappointment in projects. Frustration or impatience.

THREE OF STAVES

Keywords: Successful enterprises, planning

The woman travels and finally arrives at a calm sea framed by three staves. Reflected within the sea's depths are the first fiery rays of the sun, symbolizing the emotional resolve that enables the woman to act with intent. Her intentions are as pure as the white gown she wears; the red belt around her waist represents energy that transforms intention into creation. Grasping one of the three staves, the woman contemplates her plans; she is waiting for her ships to come in, knowing they will bring the success and the bountiful treasures so loved by the goddess Freyja.

Meanings: An enterprise about to cumulate in success. The ability to transform goals into realistic action. Business success after a successful launching. Activity with clear intent.

Reversed or weakly aspected: Ambitious plans which may not be grounded in reality. A frustrating delay in receiving success.

FOUR OF STAVES

Keywords: Stability, creating a home

The woman finds four staves securely planted upon a grassy hill.
These staves are joined together at their tops with bounteous gar-
lands dotted with red roses; they suggest the stable foundation of
a happy home. Within the four staves' perimeters, the woman is
joined by her beloved. To them, these four staves represent the
first flowering of their vision. Together they dance to celebration

and success. In the distance Asgard, the mythic castle that serves as home to Freyja, can be seen, symbolizing the ideal home all aspire to create.

Meanings: Stability of ventures. A new home. Accomplishing goals, and enjoying them with satisfaction. First success of a new venture. Putting down roots. Possibly a marriage or domestic partnership. Helpful structure.

Reversed or weakly aspected: The desire to put down roots, but elusiveness in doing so. Wanting stability. Frustrations or disappointments at home.

FIVE OF STAVES

Keywords: Conflict, competition, dissension

In a dream, the woman sees five conflicting aspects of herself, each
one a warrior armed with a stave. They use these to fight amongst
themselves in a broiling hot desert landscape. The intense rays of
the sun heats everyone's tempers, making it all the more difficult
to distinguish what the fight is really about — after all, aren't they
on the same team? When she finally wakes, the woman feels

frustrated by her limitations. She wonders what to do but feels too proud to ask for assistance.

Meanings: Inability to focus or move. Dissension, which may be within the psyche or personified in the people around you. Conflict for the sake of conflict. Ego-oriented competition. Losing sight of what's important because of petty disagreements.

Reversed or weakly aspected: Moving beyond petty concerns and worries to understand what's important. Unifying forces. Overcoming obstacles.

SIX OF STAVES

Keywords: Victory, acknowledgement, honor

Finally, a resolution is created. In triumph, the woman rides a docile horse adorned with red and white; these dressings are embroidered with gold, the precious metal most sacred to Freyja. As the woman shares the news of her victory, she is surrounded by six staves, one which bears the laurels of victory; another which is placed upon her brow, anointing her. These six staves are raised in tribute to her stamina and courage in the face of adversary.

Meanings: Victory! Enjoying success after much hard work and struggle. Acknowledgement and honor from those around you. The fruits of courage and integrity. Integration and harmony.

Reversed or weakly aspected: Victory is elusive. You've done the work, you deserve the honors, but they haven't come — perhaps because of a lack of awareness in those around you.

SEVEN OF STAVES

Keywords: Defense, combat, struggle

Attacked by six staves, the woman is trapped at the edge of a dangerous cliff. She is forced to defend herself against her will using a seventh stave. Despite the clear blue sky that curves over the landscape beneath her, the hot sun scorches the woman. Unable to get out of the heat, she feels attacked on both sides, front and back. While she has a position of advantage in this struggle, she needs to draw upon the assimilating energies of the goddess Freyja to ultimately win the battle.

Meanings: Instability and struggle. While you may have the ultimate advantage in this situation, there is still conflict. Success is possible, but only after dealing with difficult people who oppose your plans. Remember, they have their own agendas to consider. **Reversed or weakly aspected:** Indecisiveness in the face of opposition. Feeling overwhelmed. Creating problems for oneself in order to distract from what is really going on.

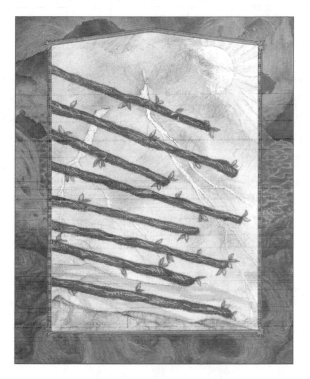

EIGHT OF STAVES

Keywords: Sudden communications, movement

From the edge of the cliff, the woman suddenly sees eight staves positioned like lightning from the heavens. These staves move like electricity, bringing important news and communications. Their message is one of excitement; of help and rescue; of fortuitous timing and information that brim with truths. These staves crack across a dramatic sky filled with storm clouds, bringing the needed release promised by the sun, which is partially hidden from view.

Meanings: Energetic movement. Quickness and suddenness. Important communications—unexpected telephone calls, surprise letters—which release uncertainties and end waiting. Unknown information finally released that makes sense.

Reversed or weakly aspected: Waiting too long for communication. Perhaps it is time to take the initiative to create waves. Stop waiting for others to make the first move.

NINE OF STAVES

Keywords: Responsibility, separation, exhaustion

Finally the woman understands—but she also understands how much work she needs to do to complete the vision she wants to share with the world. Temporarily protected by a wall of staves, the woman rests for a moment to catch her breath and struggle with her feelings of overwhelming responsibility. There is so much to consider before success can be reached. But first, the woman's thoughts and plans must be regrouped before she can continue.

Meanings: A pause in work to rest, to reconsider plans. Completion is so close, yet so far away! Need for protection or separation from others who may not be fully supportive in order to finish a project. Exhaustion or overresponsibility.

Reversed or weakly aspected: Feeling overwhelmed by work. Need for a break. Denial of responsibilities. Not fully acknowledging the work needed to finish a project.

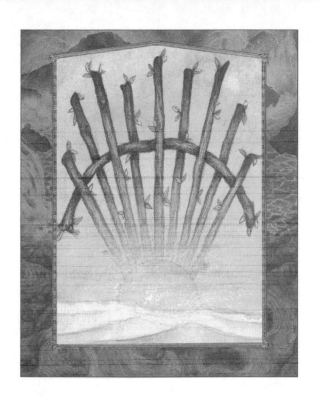

TEN OF STAVES

Keywords: Cumulation, success, creativity

From her place of protection the woman sees a glorious sunset, promising her victory. Within this sunset radiates ten staves, each symbolizing the creative promise of Freyja. Their green leaves show that they are natural extensions of the sun's warm, life-giving force—the force that symbolizes the dynamic portion of the Divine Feminine that encourages growth. While it is affirming to see the bounty promised by it, there is so much energy that it's almost too much to take in without feeling burned by its power.

Meanings: The cumulation of the creative venture begun with the one of staves. Success that becomes overwhelming with its responsibility. The final vision is within reach, but work can be oppressive.

Reversed or weakly aspected: Overwhelmed and burdened by responsibilities. No time to enjoy success—there's too much work to do!

PRINCE OF STAVES

Keywords: New ideas, communications

The Prince of Staves is the bearer of important messages that will either jolt one into action or bring recognition of what can be accomplished, using the wisdom of Freyja. He walks in a rocky landscape and holds a leafy staff to support himself. A passionate wind, symbolic of the enthusiastic ideas he loves to share, blows his brilliant red cloak about. Unfortunately, he is too young to be able to carry out his ideas—but he is able to inspire others to action.

Meanings: Important communications. Need to listen to inspiration, new ideas. However, these should be weighed according to practicality. An inexperienced young person who may be very passionate but not very pragmatic because of inexperience.

Reversed or weakly aspected: Too much energy and not enough focus. Ideas and messages that fizzle out after initial enthusiasm. Inconsistency. Overenthusiasm for the sake of emotional display.

PRINCESS OF STAVES

Keywords: Passion, integrity, action

The Princess of Staves, a fiery-haired young woman crowned with a circle of gold, vows to be as stalwart as the rocks surrounding her. Her passionate example is an inspiration to live with integrity, intent, and without compromise. About to reach all of life's fullness, and embracing all its possibilities, she glorifies Freyja's values of beauty and hard work. The Princess of Staves' ability to go forth into the world with her work exemplifies the expansive quality of confidence at its life-affirming best.

Meanings: The ability to create beauty that has use in the world. Energy, integrity, and creativity. Initiative. New ideas or ventures that must be acted upon immediately. A young woman who inspires others to live this mission.

Reversed or weakly aspected: Scattered energy. Inability to focus on matters at hand. Need to develop skills to bring dreams into reality. Too much energy or not enough energy.

KING OF STAVES

Keywords: Enthusiasm, mastery, support

Seated upon his throne and dressed in heavy robes decorated with golden embroidery depicting the sun, the King of Staves is the epitome of the sun's power. His regal, expansive, and energizing personality creates opportunities where none existed before. His authority enables him to make sure these opportunities will reach fruition. The King of Staves has the happy talent of inspiring growth in others through the warmth of his supportive friend-ship and enthusiasm.

Meanings: Dynamic, stable enthusiasm. Mastery over business ventures. The ability to bring ideas to fruition. Someone who sym-bolizes these strengths. Creative inspiration and help.

Reversed or weakly aspected: Wanting to harness these forces, but not quite strong enough to do so. Someone who seems supportive, but when push comes to shove has already lost interest.

QUEEN OF STAVES

Keywords: Power, cleverness, beauty

Power and energy is held in reserve by the beautiful, bejeweled Queen of Staves, who, like her consort, is dressed in pure white robes embroidered with golden suns. While she might seem passive as she holds court upon her rocky throne, only a moment's notice is necessary to rouse her to action. Like Freyja, the Queen of Staves' majestic qualities can inspire the creation of beauty through practical applications; she also possesses the cleverness to implement these ideas herself.

Meanings: Intelligence applied to creating material goods, business expansion. Cleverness. A woman who embodies these ideas and inspires action from others. Wit and wisdom. Enthusiasm and action. Support.

Reversed or weakly aspected: Waiting too long to use your forces. Not showing the world your talents. Undermining your authority. Lack of self-worth or low self-esteem.

THE SUIT OF SWORDS
The Path of Isis

Element: Air, salt

Corresponds to Magic, major arcana card number 1

The suit of swords is associated with Isis, the Egyptian fertility goddess. Swords symbolize the incisive forces of the intellect— they cut through and focus the energy grown in the preceding suit of staves. Think of swords as the shears that prune weak branches from the sapling tree so that it can strengthen and bear fruit; this pruning may seem severe but ultimately it is a necessary life-giving action.

Swords also symbolize the Divine Feminine's magical ability to transform painful situations into areas of personal growth. The story of the goddess Isis and her consort Osiris illustrates this affirming principle beautifully. Like Isis, we can choose how to use our swords: we can turn them against ourselves when we are in pain. Or we can transform the situation through knowledge and understanding, the better to personify the all-encompassing wisdom of the Divine Feminine.

THE MYTH OF ISIS ✦ ✦ ✦

The story of Isis shows us the transformative powers of love, grief, death, and rebirth. For over three thousand years—from before 3000 B.C. to the second century A.D.—Isis was worshiped in Egypt as the Great Mother Goddess of the Universe. Isis looked after the affairs of the day while her sister, Nephthys, took care of the night. She also had two brothers, Osiris and Set. Osiris was responsible for the fertile soil, and Set ruled the barren desert. When they were old enough, the sun god Ra married Isis to Osiris and Set to Nephthys. Isis and Osiris were blissful in their love and were adored by many; no moon could compare to the bliss of their passion, no sun to the brightness of their honor. Set noticed this and jealousy ate at his soul, giving him no rest. So he entrapped his brother in a coffin and heaved him into the swirling waters of the Nile.

Griefstricken, Isis transformed herself into a dark bird and flew everywhere searching for Osiris. Finally, she found the coffin embedded in a tree. Isis hid the coffin from Set. But Set learned all and he mercilessly cut Osiris' body into fourteen pieces and scattered them in all four directions.

Isis was not deterred. She traveled up and down the Nile in a papyrus boat, searching for the pieces of her lost husband and brother. When she had found them all, she placed them next to each other and, with the power of her love, she briefly brought her husband back to life. That last act of love resulted in Isis conceiving a child, Horus, the falcon-headed god. Together, Isis and Horus were able to bring Set to justice for the murder of Osiris.

✦ ✦ ✦

ACE OF SWORDS

Keywords: Wisdom, understanding, intelligence

A grey sky reveals a desolate desert landscape set with pyramids, the final resting place of the monarchs of ancient Egypt. Within a mound of sand stands a single sword — its defiant presence challenges those who would wield it to gain the riches stored within the pyramids. The sword's ornate gold handle is decorated with the horned symbol of Isis, the Egyptian goddess of wisdom and fertility; it is shaped like the lotus, the flower of spiritual enlightenment. But it is the sword's sharp blade that bears the symbol of the Divine Feminine, whose incisive powers of intellect it represents.

Meanings: The incisive powers of the Divine Feminine. Pure understanding and wisdom. The ability to wield your "sword" wisely. Clarity and good judgment. Knowing the difference between right and wrong. Truth. Intelligence. Beginning of a cycle of intellectual growth.

Reversed or weakly aspected: Need for thought. Are you using your swords against yourself or as a tool for growth? Self-recrimination and rejection of personal power to blame others. Confusion.

TWO OF SWORDS

Keywords: Peace, truce, impasse

An impasse is met. To better look within herself, the woman has blindfolded herself; this way she will not be confused by other's opinions or too much information. As she sits surrounded by lotus flowers, the Nile River flows behind her, symbolizing the confusing emotions she has turned her back upon for now. The perfection of the woman's inner balance is symbolized by the two swords she

127

has balanced within her arms; if she needs them they are there to be used, but for now all is peaceful.

Meanings: Peaceful truce. Balance attained, but eventually issues will have to be confronted. Understanding a difficult situation. Inability to change; the ability to accept. Emotional control.

Reversed or weakly aspected: Discomfort with a decision. Overreliance on intellect, leaving emotions unconsidered. Uncomfortable relationships.

THREE OF SWORDS

Keywords: Heartbreak, grief, oversensitivity

Floating in a grey sky, a heart is pierced by three swords. Through the introspection of loss, these three swords offer wisdom and understanding. This wounded heart also bears the eye of Isis superimposed upon it, representing the sorrow experienced by Isis upon the death of Osiris. The stormy sky surrounding it threatens rain, which cleanses and brings release, like tears to a griefstricken soul. Despite everything, all is not lost — the symbol of the Divine Feminine is also etched upon the heart, promising compassion and healing to all.

Meanings: A sharp pain to the heart — disappointment, end of a love relationship, separation. Sorrow that can enlighten or debilitate. Oversensitivity. Time for healing. The need to transform grief into understanding.

Reversed or weakly aspected: Overindulging in grief for the sake of drama. Identifying with the drama rather than the loss. Slow easing of sorrow.

FOUR OF SWORDS

Keywords: Healing, introspection, meditation

In order to heal herself, the woman rests upon a pallet hidden among rushes; embroidered upon her royal purple bedclothes is the horned symbol of Isis. As the woman recuperates, four swords are magically suspended above her amid a swirling starry sky. They protect her from the outside world, allowing her the space and time she needs to fully regain her strength. In time, the woman will be as strong as Isis, and will be able to transform her problems through the strength of her understanding. But for now, she needs rest.

Meanings: Introspection. Solitude. Need time to heal or rest. Detachment from the everyday world to regain balance. Recuperation from illness. Take a break from stressful situations.
Reversed or weakly aspected: Enforced isolation. Loneliness. More recovery time needed than what has been allowed. Needing more time alone.

FIVE OF SWORDS

Keywords: Discomfort, struggle

Completely rested and healed from her time alone, the woman
moves on. She arrives at an arid landscape where five heavy
swords have been abandoned. Two of these swords have been laid
down in a position of surrender. But she doesn't trust this offering
fully: as she scans the distance for enemies, she collects three
swords within her arms, one which she places in her right hand in

readiness. If necessary, she will be as fierce as the goddess Isis in her search for vengeance.

Meanings: An uncomfortable truce—but is the conflict really over? "Arming" oneself just in case of attack. Lack of trust. Possible defeat, or feelings of defeat. Discomfort or struggle with a situation. The need for self-protection.

Reversed or weakly aspected: Disingenuous surrender. Defeat because of indecisiveness. Paranoia. Dishonesty.

SIX OF SWORDS

Keywords: Transitions, travel, movement

The woman, looking like Isis as she searched for Osiris along the Nile, is traveling in a boat to a better place. She has gathered six swords to take with her; these symbolize the new understanding and clarity that she will use in her new life, where she can fully utilize the wisdom of the Divine Feminine. Above her fly two dark birds; they are the harbingers of understanding, flying and swooping just out of reach as they lead her toward wisdom and understanding.

Meanings: Transitions that go smoothly. New knowledge that helps one grow and move beyond current limitations. The lessening of difficulties. Travel in order to gain distance from difficulties. Detachment so as to better understand a situation. Healing.

Reversed or weakly aspected: More understanding of a situation is needed before it can change. Delay in departures, travel.

SEVEN OF SWORDS

Keywords: Defense, caution, vulnerability

After arriving in a new land, the woman tries to carry seven
swords for protection. Only five will fit in her arms—and even
these are awkward to carry; with reluctance she will have to leave
two swords behind. As the woman nervously looks over her
shoulder, she hopes these remaining swords will not be used

against her. She feels vulnerable—if only she possessed the strength of Isis she wouldn't need all these swords.

Meanings: Feeling vulnerable. The ability to defend oneself in a difficult situation. However, energy should not be placed in recriminations. Need for caution and examination. Be careful about using words that can be turned against you.

Reversed or weakly aspected: Paranoia. Feeling defensive. Possible guilt. Need to protect oneself.

EIGHT OF SWORDS

Keywords: Depression, entrapment, self-victimization

In the distance, a storm ominously gathers. Too exhausted to continue, the woman collapses upon the desert sand. She is over-whelmed and entrapped as surely as Osiris was within the coffin. Eight swords surround her, like the steel bars of a prison cage. Despite this unpleasant image, the woman would be able to find her way to freedom if she would only lift up her eyes to see. But she is too overwhelmed by sorrow and difficulties to do so.

Meanings: Inability to move. Depression that is incapacitating. Feeling victimized or misunderstood by others. Extreme sorrow that may be cause by oversensitivity. Feeling rejection. Entrapped by emotions and sorrow.

Reversed or weakly aspected: Obsession with self and personal problems to the detriment of others. Problems that may come from within. Projecting negativity onto others. Things may not be as bad as they seem. The lessening of self-obsession and negativity.

NINE OF SWORDS

Keywords: Anxiety, unresolved issues, insomnia

There is no rest for the woman, for nightmares torment her sleep.
But while these dreams are painful, they offer her an opportunity
for catharsis. They bring up nagging worries that need to be examined. The symbol of the eye of Isis beneath the woman's
pillow reveals the divinely feminine understanding that awaits

her—for only after she understands what these worries really mean will she be released from them.

Meanings: Insomnia. Worries that keep one awake. An issue that needs to be looked at more closely; only then will it be transformed. Fear or nagging anxiety. Guilt. Psychic disturbances. Catharsis.

Reversed or weakly aspected: The fading away of these worries. Understanding. Someone close who is suffering from depression, anxiety, illness. The ability to transform pain into strength.

TEN OF SWORDS

Keywords: Understanding, endings, wisdom

Finally the woman arrives at a vantage point where she can see the meeting of earth and sky. Several lightning bolts, representing the shock of enlightenment, crack in the distant cloudy sky. In front of this intense scene, ten swords are interwoven into a graceful pattern. These swords symbolize the power of Isis; they offer magic to those who learn how to wield them. Those who understand how to wield the swords will be able to transform difficulties into wisdom that heals the self and others.

Meanings: The perfection of understanding, as expressed in the example of Isis. Wisdom gained after struggle. The ending of a difficult situation. Experience as the best teacher, for better and for worse. Sharing knowledge with others.

Reversed or weakly aspected: More needs to be considered before complete understanding can be gained. Overwhelmed by too much information— things need to be prioritized before progress can be made. Getting lost in details — the inability to "see the forest for the trees."

PRINCE OF SWORDS

Keywords: Messages, influence, articulation

Courtly but strong-willed, the Prince of Swords is able to use language as gracefully as he wields the sword clasped to his chest—there is no confusion or ambivalence in his words. Upright and honorable, he is a messenger who brings crucial information, often in the written form. A friend to writers, lawyers—those who wield words for a living—he brings clarity to situations where there was none before, wisdom where foolishness reigned.

Meanings: Articulation. News that brings sense to a situation. Messages, communications, often written. The ability to create influence and bring understanding, using the power of words. Someone who personifies this role.

Reversed or weakly aspected: Waiting for news. Feeling inarticulate, unable to stand up for oneself. Confusing messages.

PRINCESS OF SWORDS

Keywords: Decisiveness, clarity, defense

Holding her sword more as a staff of support than as a tool of defense—though if she needed to, she would certainly know how to use it—the Princess of Swords is able to cut her way through the swampy marsh of confusion. Strong-willed and filled with confidence, she is completely at one with her intentions. Other's opinions do not deter her from following the path she knows she must follow. The Princess of Swords is unstoppable—the strength of her focus gains her the admiration of many.

Meanings: The ability to move in an incisive way. Cutting through confusion. Being able to defend oneself brilliantly. Focus and clarity of understanding. A woman who symbolizes these forces.

Reversed or weakly aspected: Not understanding as much as one would like to. The desire to move, but feeling thwarted.

KING OF SWORDS

Keywords: Authority, responsibility, detachment

Sitting upon his throne surrounded by lotus blossoms, the King of Swords is able to bring the wisdom, detachment, and clarity of Isis to any situation. He is the authority able to look at a plan and recognize what is needed as well as what can be cut away for a stronger, more focused approach. Completely at home with his intellect, he is a force to be admired and ultimately reckoned with—he symbolizes the high standards we all must achieve to experience success in the world of the intellect.

Meanings: Calm authority and integrity. A helpful older man who won't sugarcoat words to protect others' feelings. Incisive intellect. Responsibility. High values that demand hard work.

Reversed or weakly aspected: Wanting authority to take over to avoid responsibility. Placing too much trust in the intellect. Being too critical.

QUEEN OF SWORDS

Keywords: Brilliance, honesty, clarity

Wearing a headpiece that bears the symbol of Isis, the Queen of Swords is a force to be reckoned with. She is the ideal woman to consult when troubled or confused with problems — she will tell it like it is, even to the point of sometimes being considered a little harsh. Strong and brilliant, the Queen of Swords rules over all aspects of intellectual understanding. She symbolizes the perfect manifestation of the Divine Feminine, gained through experiences both happy and painful.

Meanings: Dazzling intellect. Perfect understanding. The ability to clarify through language. Brilliance in writing, speaking, or anything else transmitted with words. An older woman who has these qualities.

Reversed or weakly aspected: May symbolize loss or wounds; despite good intentions, sharp words wound people and affect relationships. Allowing intellect to rule over the heart detrimentally. Psychological manipulation.

THE SUIT OF PENTACLES
The Path of Lakshmi

Element: Earth, gold

Corresponds to Fortune, major arcana card number 10

The suit of pentacles is associated with Lakshmi, the Hindu goddess of fortune and prosperity. Pentacles, as gold and shiny as the sparkling jewels Lakshmi is so fond of, symbolize the riches contained within the earth that are ours for the taking—as long as we know how to mine them.

The suit of pentacles represents the grand harvest of the Divine Feminine which arrives after we master the lessons of the three previous suits. Cups water the seed of inspiration initially planted by the Divine Feminine. Staves are the first growth that, encouraged by the sun's energy, sprout vigorously from the fertile earth. Swords prune staves for the sake of growth. Finally, in the suit of pentacles, the strong reinvigorated tree bears seeded fruit so the cycle may start anew.

Pentacles tell the story of the bounty of the earth—symbolized in so many societies as a generous earth goddess able to nurture all of her inhabitants. Lakshmi, the Hindu personification of this fertile, prosperous, and distinctly feminine force, is well loved by many Hindu to this day for these qualities.

THE MYTH OF LAKSHMI

In Hindu mythology, the goddess Lakshmi is believed to represent all that is feminine, while her consort, Vishnu, honored as the conqueror of darkness, represents all that is masculine. Lakshmi was created when Vishnu churned the wondrous Ocean of Milk; she magically appeared from its creamy depths, seated upon a lotus flower throne with a lotus blossom crown upon her pale brow, the lotus symbolizing her divine enlightenment. Lakshmi and Vishnu had a son, whom they named Kama; Kama was honored as the god of romantic love in the Hindu tradition.

As the goddess of earthly prosperity, Lakshmi is thought to be attracted to sparkling jewels, like the riches she bestows upon her faithful worshippers. In fact, some people believe that Lakshmi lives in the sky with the stars—the most beautiful jewels of all. Every year in November on the night of the new moon, when the sky is darkest and stars their brightest, a festival called Divali is celebrated in her honor. Indian women clean their homes and hang tiny lanterns as bright as diamonds, hoping to attract Lakshmi's notice, so they may win her favor for the coming year.

☛ ☛ ☛

ACE OF PENTACLES

Keywords: Fertility, generosity, prosperity

Within an enchanted landscape dotted with gold flowers, a lush tree bears a fantastic fruit—a single golden coin, symbolizing the highest and most bountiful manifestation of the Divine Feminine upon earth. This ornately decorated coin bears the image of a pentacle, the five-pointed star that is an ancient and magical symbol of protection and wisdom. Its five connected sides are thought to reveal the never ending, always flowing force of the Divine Feminine. Engraved around the pentacle is an image of a lotus blossom, representing spiritual enlightenment as well as the joyful birth of Lakshmi, the goddess of earthly prosperity.

Meanings: The Divine Feminine's purest evocation of prosperity, fertility, and generosity. The beginning of a new phase of life that promises the good fortune of Lakshmi. Attainment of material goals as well as contentment in personal life. Fertility. Pleasures of the material world.

Reversed or weakly aspected: A desire to reap the fruits of labor. Elusive success. Need to examine how one undermines oneself.

TWO OF PENTACLES

Keywords: Grace, expansion, juggling

By the sea, the woman gracefully juggles two pentacles. She is so completely focused upon her act, so undistracted by outside influences, that she does not drop the pentacles even as they swirl in mid-air. Around her feet—clad in green, the color of earthly manifestation—flows the incoming tide; this symbolizing the perfect balance she holds within herself. Around her blows a gentle wind, representing the twin forces of change and movement.

Meanings: The ability to juggle several situations at once—jobs, opportunities, ideas. Balance between the earthly and the spiritual worlds. Grace and bounty. Commerce and expansion.

Reversed or weakly aspected: Taking on too much for now. Feeling overwhelmed by demands. Time to concentrate on one thing at a time; do this well before you expand. Overcommitting oneself.

THREE OF PENTACLES

Keywords: Building, material manifestation

The woman comes to a palatial building, the most beautiful she has ever seen. The golden light from the sky highlights three magnificent pentacles, which are suspended within the structure of the building's bell-shaped roof. The woman can tell that this palace is the cumulation of much hard work and talent, as well as material goods and constructive planning. To her, it symbolizes the goals that she can reach if she works hard and draws upon the wisdom of Lakshmi.

Meanings: Constructive and pragmatic building — career, relationships, home. Alchemy, or turning base energy into gold. The ability to transform talents into material goods or business success. Cooperating with others to create such a venture.

Reversed or weakly aspected: Need to develop one's talents before entering the marketplace. Recheck plans for expansion — are they practical? Are they appropriate for your abilities? Time for a reality check from those who may be more experienced.

FOUR OF PENTACLES

Keywords: Wealth, stability, security

Pleased with herself, the woman rests in a peaceful meadow surrounded by purple mountains—the mountains symbolizing spiritual enlightenment and the meadow, earthly manifestation. She is draped in richly embroidered robes, laden with jewels, decorated with gold—as glittering with wealth as the goddess Lakshmi herself. Surrounded by four pentacles, the woman is the epitome of luxury and earthly prosperity.

Meanings: Wealth and prosperity. Stability of material forces in one's life. Holding onto worldly goods. An family inheritance — this could be a talent handed down, money, land, or a quality that adds richness to life. Self-satisfaction.

Reversed or weakly aspected: Possibility of being miserly with wealth, talents. Or, conversely, being an overly generous spend-thrift. Need to conserve and protect resources.

FIVE OF PENTACLES

Keywords: Poverty, sterility, insecurity

Wrapped in rags, two beggars wander through a snowy landscape in search of aid. The snow and winds are so fierce that one of the women covers her face against the harsh cold. She wonders if she will ever again feel warmth, security, and prosperity—all the comforting things she associates with the goddess Lakshmi. The other woman tries not to fret; instead, she looks up at the snow and sees its pure, transcendent beauty.

Meanings: An experience of poverty that forces one to look within for greater resources. This poverty may be personified as a lack of wealth or in a sense of emotional sterility. Spiritual impoverishment. Feeling deprived. Insecurity.

Reversed or weakly aspected: These feelings are transitory. Have faith in the future—a more prosperous phase of life is on its way. The ability to make the best of a difficult situation.

SIX OF PENTACLES

Keywords: Generosity, helping others

Two beggars meet up with the woman, still dressed in the rich jewels and robes of the wealthy. Moved by their plight, she decides to help them and share her wealth with them. Luckily, the woman is so prosperous that the act of giving only adds to her prosperity. However, the dynamic of giving and receiving makes her uncomfortable, since it implies a debt on the part of the beggars; she knows that true generosity involves no strings or expectations of return.

Meanings: True generosity and philanthropy. Sharing talents with the world, and hoping they'll be received gracefully. Trusting in the prosperity of the universe. Helping others who are less fortunate without expectations or obligations.

Reversed or weakly aspected: Jealousy or envy from those less fortunate. Not giving with a pure heart. Need for appreciation. Using wealth to manipulate others.

SEVEN OF PENTACLES

Keywords: Waiting, expectations, nurturing

In hopes of creating even more prosperity, the woman tends a
growing tree. She weeds around its roots and prunes its heavy
boughs so it may grow better. As she waits for its fruit—here symbolized by seven golden pentacles growing upon its strong
branches—to ripen, she thinks back over all her nurturing. The

woman looks forward to enjoying the richly deserved harvest she has worked toward for so long.

Meanings: Expectations of reward. Waiting for a harvest—be that a creative project, money, personal relationship, or any venture that time and work is invested in—to occur. Tending your "garden." Nurturing others.

Reversed or weakly aspected: Impatience. Insecurity about whether the reward received for the work rendered will be worth it. Need to work harder to create prosperity.

EIGHT OF PENTACLES

Keywords: Talent, compensation, honorable work

The woman decides to express her artistry by painting a golden pentacle upon a silk canvas. As she works, she loses herself in creativity's flow; she feels blessed as she draws upon the talents given to her by the Divine Feminine. Symbolizing the golden circle of contentment the woman has created through her focused and honorable labor, an arc of seven pentacles appears above her head, like a golden rainbow depicting the material rewards of Lakshmi.

Meanings: Creative work. Fair payment for hard work. Meeting deadlines. Developing talents for the marketplace. Working with integrity and discipline. The appearance of this card in a reading for an artist or craftsperson is an affirmation of skill and talent.

Reversed or weakly aspected: Avoiding work. Need to bring talents to the next level of skill—perhaps taking time for vocational training or school. Unhappiness with money received for work given. Involvement in "get rich quick" schemes as a way of avoiding the reality of hard labor.

NINE OF PENTACLES

Keywords: Luxury, prosperity, pleasure

After completing her labor and bringing it to the marketplace, the woman arrives at an enchanted garden. Overflowing with perfumed flowers, jasmine trees, and singing birds, she luxuriates in all the beauty and pleasure she has worked so hard to create. The blessings of Lakshmi are symbolized by the nine pentacles that appear around her, like fruit upon the vine of earthly delights. She feels the presence of the Divine Feminine all around her.

Meanings: Pleasure or sensuality. Feeling blessed by life. Enjoying the fruits of one's labors. Fertility and luxury. Material prosperity—now that this has been accomplished, perhaps it is time to create a family.

Reversed or weakly aspected: Overindulgence in material pleasures, perhaps to the point of compromising financial stability. Guilt over having so much; inability to enjoy it. Fear of other's envy.

TEN OF PENTACLES

Keywords: Cumulation, prosperity, expansion

The gateway from the enchanted garden leads to a lovely verdant landscape. Ten pentacles glitter within its ornate carvings and upon a tree, showing the inherent expansiveness of the world—all the wonderful things sacred to Lakshmi, the goddess of prosperity. There is more than enough for all to enjoy. Here the suit of pentacles is expressed in its strongest form—showing the benevolent promise of the Divine Feminine at its most expansive.

Meanings: Great satisfaction. Prosperity and the construction of a home that reflects this state. Creating a family to share wealth with. The successful cumulation of business plans. Expansion. An inheritance. Joy and pleasure.

Reversed or weakly aspected: Discontent at home or difficulties with family relationships. Wanting greater prosperity, but uncertain how to achieve it. Despite coming close, success on the material plane is elusive.

PRINCE OF PENTACLES

Keywords: Business ideas, messages, education

Garbed in embroidered silks, gold, and jewels, the Prince of
Pentacles holds a single magnificent pentacle in his hands. He is a
pragmatic force, able to gain the knowledge needed to bring a plan
to fruition. Practical and grounded, he is surprisingly mature for
his young years and is not afraid to work hard in order to manifest
the earthly prosperity so blessed by Lakshmi. When not working,

he can be a bringer of messages and ideas, able to show where businesses can expand and when they can harvest.

Meanings: Gaining the knowledge necessary to make an idea a reality. Education. Business ideas, deals. Practical planning. Mail or messages that bring possibilities for expansion. Money on the way. Business opportunities.

Reversed or weakly aspected: Too much time thinking, not enough doing. Business deals that need to be examined closely. Waiting for money, business news. Unrealistic planning.

PRINCESS OF PENTACLES

Keywords: Opportunities, hard work, development

Seductive and sweetly perfumed, the Princess of Pentacles offers all of life's bounties. Her presence reminds others of the hard work and clear focus involved in gaining these riches. To possess these, though, desire is not enough — constructive action must be taken. The Princess of Pentacles, as a personification of the practical active aspect of the goddess Lakshmi, is able to provide the impetus to move toward creating these opportunities.

Meanings: The ability, hard work, and wisdom necessary for creating opportunities for growth, beauty. Movement in this direction. The ability to work hard to create prosperity. Taking care of the self on the material level, and enjoying the pleasures associated with this. A woman who personifies these forces.

Reversed or weakly aspected: Inertia or laziness. Not taking action or responsibilities. Oversensuality. Wanting to get something for nothing—credit where no credit is due.

KING OF PENTACLES

Keywords: Steadfastness, wealth creation, riches

Crowned and enthroned with the best the world has to offer, the
King of Pentacles is a majestic, stabilizing force with the ability to
bring business or real estate deals to completion. He is the money-
man behind the scenes, the nurturing authority whose steadfast
integrity inspires others as they create their own businesses.

His practical wisdom is an inspiration to all who would own the earthly prosperity that Lakshmi and the Divine Feminine promise.

Meanings: The forces of worldly prosperity. The ability to create wealth. Real estate transactions. Investments—money or emotional. Steadfast. Someone who personifies these forces.

Reversed or weakly aspected: Unstable, pie-in-the-sky business deals. Need to be more realistic. Involvement with people who may promise more than they are able to deliver. The need for stability and discipline in life.

QUEEN OF PENTACLES

Keywords: Fertility, prosperity, beauty

The Queen of Pentacles is the very personification of the fertile life force of the Divine Feminine. Like the jewels she wears and the pentacle posed upon her lap, she bears all the riches and possibilities of the physical world. This expansive, joyful older woman has the happy talent to create heaven upon earth. The archetypal earth mother, the Queen of Pentacles is the physical manifestation of the goddess Lakshmi upon earth; she brings harmony and beauty to all who pass her way.

Meanings: Fertility, possibly parenthood. Creating prosperity and harmony. Beauty, wealth, the home. Regality. Warmth and affection. Love. Happy harmonious home. A woman who is nurturing and accepting.

Reversed or weakly aspected: Need to ground oneself. Perhaps an overmaterialistic orientation to life. Disappointment in the home, or lack of focus upon.

Part Three:
USING *THE GODDESS TAROT*

CARD SPREADS WITH
THE GODDESS TAROT

The tarot has been used for many years by people striving to better understand their life journey. In my book, *Embracing the Goddess Within*, I write of the challenge of acknowledging the divine within ourselves. I would like to think that *The Goddess Tarot* can be used as a tool for this great quest.

For those who fear the tarot or invest it with predictive powers outside theirselves, rest easy. I believe that tarot readings cannot tell you what you do not already know, even if you are unwilling to accept this knowledge at this time. A good tarot reading should be an adventure into truth seeking rather than soothsaying. The beauty of tarot is that it presents this information in a new form—like another opinion, but one without a vested interest.

For these reasons and others, most people utilize the wisdom of the tarot by placing a number of cards into a pattern called a spread. Each card position within the spread symbolizes an area of the question to be explored during the tarot reading.

PREPARING FOR A TAROT READING ✦ ✦ ✦

Before a tarot reading starts, a question needs to be decided upon. How to phrase this question is an important consideration.

Generally, questions that receive the best responses are those which are posed with the greatest thought and clarity of intentions. Choose your words carefully; wording is important and implies an awareness of the responsibility involved.

Next the tarot cards for the spread are chosen. Cards are usually chosen for a tarot reading by shuffling the cards a preordained number of times (to assure randomness) and cutting the deck. Some tarot readers prefer to shuffle their cards themselves, allowing the querant (the person who is asking the question) to only handle the deck while cutting it; they feel this allows them to be more intimate with their cards. Other readers prefer to have the querant choose their cards themselves, believing the querant will choose the most appropriate cards for their situation.

Another thing to consider before you choose your cards is whether you wish to include reversed (or upside-down) cards in your readings. These can be created by turning some of the cards around as you shuffle. Some people believe that reversed cards add another dimension of clarity to readings; these cards serve as focal points, showing where energy may be blocked in a situation or special attention needed. Others feel that all the information needed to create a full picture is already contained within the 78 cards of the tarot — reversed cards just muddy the water. Again, this is up to you.

However you decide to proceed, it is important to focus yourself before the actual reading. A simple ritual, such as lighting a candle or closing your eyes for a moment, can help create a properly receptive atmosphere to the information about to be shared by the cards.

Following are descriptions and diagrams for four tarot spreads. Each one offers a different way for you to explore *The Goddess Tarot*.

Whichever spread you decide to use, as you look over the cards chosen for your reading, try to think of each card as a chapter in a story you are telling. What do the pictures tell you? How can this story be changed, if change is wanted? And what lesson is being taught, what challenge offered?

Also, note the proximity and position of a card, and whether there is a preponderance of any one suit or arcana. Personal feelings or memories may surface as you gaze at the images before you—they are important and should be noted as well.

ᕽ ᕽ ᕽ

The Goddess Tarot Oracle

The simplest spread—and a good way to familiarize yourself with each card in *The Goddess Tarot*—is to choose one card from the deck while concentrating on your question or the issue at hand. To do this, place the deck face down and pick a card randomly from within the deck. Or, shuffle the deck, cut it, and choose the top card.

Consider this card an oracle granting you the information you need at that moment. You may even meditate upon the chosen card–the same way you would an especially complex dream–using its images and symbols as a focal point for self-examination.

While you could use any card for this exercise, working with the major arcana alone is a wonderful opportunity to learn about each goddess represented in *The Goddess Tarot* and the divinely feminine experience she represents.

A variation of this exercise is to spread the entire deck out face up upon a flat surface. Take a deep breath to quiet any thoughts or worries which may distract you. As you examine each card, take note of the card you are most attracted to and why. This card can be used also as a tool for meditation practice or self-examination.

֍ ֍ ֍

The Past/Present/Future Spread

Slightly more complex than The Goddess Tarot Oracle is the Past/Present/Future spread. This is a good spread to use for simple questions. It's also great when you're short of time but need a quick overview of a situation.

Choose four cards at random from your deck and lay them out as shown in the diagram. Each card is placed face down; it is turned up as it is examined:

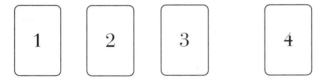

Card 1: This card represents the past, or foundation, of the matter being considered.

Card 2: The present, or as things stand now.

Card 3: The possible future, if things continue as they are now. Remember, the future can be influenced by our attitudes, actions, and intentions.

Card 4: The final card offers the overall message, or lesson, of the spread, summing up everything examined so far.

The Celtic Cross Spread

Perhaps because of its versatile ability to cover many aspects of a situation in great depth, the Celtic Cross is a staple of tarot spreads. For this reading, give yourself at least twenty minutes (or longer, if possible).

The first step in creating the Celtic Cross is to choose a card from the deck to signify the querant. There are several ways to do this. Traditional ways include selecting a court card—prince, princess, king, or queen—according to the age, sex, and coloring of the querant; for example, a young woman with light hair would be represented by the Princess of Cups, an older man with red hair, the King of Staves.

Another way is to chose the major arcana card associated with the goddess who has influence over the matter being examined. For example, use the goddess Venus as represented in the Love card (number VI) for queries regarding love relationships; use the goddess Tara (Beginnings, Number 0) if your question is about new ventures.

After the significator card is decided upon, the deck is shuffled, cut, and ten cards are chosen from the top. They are placed in order of appearance as shown in the diagram, with the significator beneath card #1.

As shown and explained on the following page, each card in the Celtic Cross Spread represents one area of the question or issue being examined in the reading.

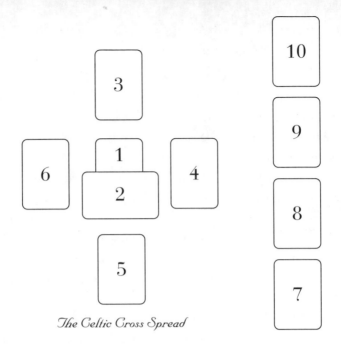

The Celtic Cross Spread

Card 1: The overall situation, or atmosphere, surrounding the querant in regards to the question.

Card 2: What is influencing the situation for better or for worse. What needs to be considered.

Card 3: The foundation of the issue.

Card 4: The past, or influence that is now passing away.

Card 5: What is on the querant's mind at this time.

Card 6: Near future, or the influence now coming into play.

Card 7: How the querant sees the situation, or how it is influencing them at this time.

Card 8: How others view the querant in this situation; ways they may help or hinder.

Card 9: Hopes and fears; the emotions surrounding the querant regarding the situation.

Card 10: Possible outcome, if things continue on the path now taken. This is a reflection of the current moment in time and can change depending upon the course of action taken.

❧ ❧ ❧

The Relationship Cross Spread

This spread, taught to me by veteran tarot reader Melanie Hope Greenberg, is valuable for exploring complex questions where two people are involved. What is especially good about the Relationship Cross is that three cards are used to sum up each area explored, allowing a more complete picture than can be created with a single card.

This spread is also unusual because of the order in which the cards are examined: instead of reading from the first card chosen to the last, cards are read according to group position.

Give yourself at least thirty minutes to explore the multifaceted aspects of this spread. After shuffling and cutting the deck, choose thirteen cards from the top and place them according to the diagram.

When reading this spread, first examine cards 13 though 11, which represents the past. Then move onto cards 1 though 3, or the querant in present time. Next look at cards 5 through 7, which represent the other person in the situation. Cards 8 through 10 show the future as it may appear according to the way the situation is now being played out. Finally, card 4 should be looked at for an overview of the reading.

The Relationship Cross Spread

Cards 1 through 3: These cards represent the querant and
their present role in the relationship.

Card 4: Represents the outcome of the question regarding
the relationship.

Cards 5 through 7: These cards represent the other person
involved in the relationship and their current situation.

Cards 8 through 10: The future of the relationship, if things
continue as they are.

Cards 11 through 13: The past or history of the relationship and
how it has affected the present situation.

Tarot spreads are as varied as the issues examined that can be
examined within them. As you work with *The Goddess Tarot*, I hope
you will feel free to expand upon these or customize them to suit
your needs. Use them as a springboard for your own creativity;
create your own vision!

SAMPLE READINGS
USING *THE GODDESS TAROT*

A book can only take you so far: it is only through working with *The Goddess Tarot* that you can truly learn the multidimensional aspects of the Devine Feminine offered by these cards. Here are a few final thoughts to help you achieve more satisfying tarot readings.

As you continue with *The Goddess Tarot*, feel free to take only what rings true to your personal experiences as your own, and leave behind what doesn't. Do not be afraid to personalize what remains so that it resonates for you. During readings, take note of any feelings, thoughts, or reactions you may experience—these will add a level of emotional richness that no book definition can provide.

It is also important to honor your intuition. For it is here that the quiet wisdom of the Divine Feminine often speaks loudest to those with the willingness to hear.

Another helpful exercise I recommend is to record your tarot readings in a journal. Often the conscious act of writing down this information will jog the subconscious into making connections previously missed. And looking back over recorded readings often highlights repeated themes which can only become obvious after enough time has passed.

Most of the time you will probably find your readings to be astonishingly clear, requiring only a simple examination to let its full picture unfold. If the meaning of a tarot reading seems mysterious, perhaps the situation itself is confused. It may not be the correct time for the the information to be given — wait a little while before trying again. And finally, remember that the future is fluid and is affected by our actions in the present.

What follows are some transcripts of actual readings done using *The Goddess Tarot* — I hope they inspire you as you work with these cards. As I read for these people, I emphasized the psychological aspects of their readings over the predictive. While some identifying details have been changed here to protect the privacy of the people involved, the cards chosen and the essential character of the readings are unchanged.

∽ ∽ ∽

Sample Reading #1: The Goddess Tarot Oracle

While working on this book, I decided to pick one card to sum up my experiences writing it. I chose Magic, associated with the goddess Isis. Since I had recently decided to take a more proactive stance in my career, this card seemed an affirmation that I was

Sample Reading # 1
The Goddess Tarot Oracle

indeed moving in the right direction. Isis' protective stance and regal attitude made me feel that I need to play the role of guardian to my creative work even more stringently; so often artists and authors fail recognize the material and spiritual value of their work in the world. And the myth of Isis reminded me that my magic is within me; it can be called into action at any time to empower myself as I worked on this book.

ഐ ഐ ഐ

Sample Reading #2:
The Past / Present / Future Spread

Kate, an attractive 50-ish gift shop owner, wanted to know if she was following her spiritual path. Since we were short on time, we chose the Past/Present/Future Spread. After looking over the cards, I answered a resounding *yes*. I was amazed by all the Major Arcana cards that showed up — three out of four cards.

Card 1: In her past, I could see Kate had experienced some sort of recovery (Four of Swords). She admitted having had an emotional breakdown that forced her to look hard at herself and her life.

Card 2: To represent her present life, Kate choose the Major Arcana card Wisdom. She seeks the spiritual path symbolized by the

1	2	3	4
Four of Swords	II Wisdom	XX Judgment	XXI The World

Sample Reading # 2:
The Past/Present/Future Spread

Hindu goddess Sarasvati and is actively trying to incorporate her new knowledge into her life's work.

Card 3: In her future, Kate wants to move live her life in a more greatly authoritative way, trusting herself more and depending less on the caprices of others — especially in her work situation. The Major Arcana card Judgment (associated with Gwenhwyfar, a sovereign goddess) suggests she will be able to do so. She will also serve as role model to others by her example.

Card 4: The card Kate chose to represent her overall situation is The World, associated with the earth goddess Gaia. By incorporating spiritual values into her work environment, she hopes her gift shop will bring the best that earth and heaven can offer: enlightenment and material success.

✢ ✢ ✢

Sample Reading #3:
The Celtic Cross

This is a record of a reading I gave Anne, a 34 year-old physical therapist. Her question was about where a love relationship was heading; the man she was involved with was in the middle of resolving a previous relationship. While he and Anne were happy together, she couldn't help but feel he wasn't fully available and wondered if she was setting herself up for a broken heart.

The first thing I noticed while looking at the cards Anne chose was the preponderance of pentacles, staves, and court cards. The presence of only one Major Arcana card suggested that while her current situation was frustrating, it wasn't a huge problem, just

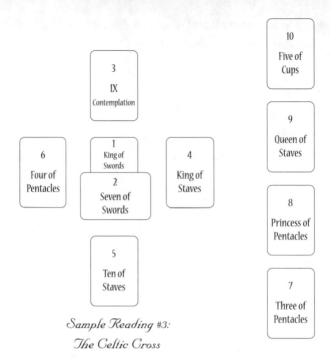

Sample Reading #3:
The Celtic Cross

part of life's complex fabric. I also explained to her about the goddesses Freyja and Lakshmi, who feature so prominently in the suits of staves and pentacles. Freyja, representing the forces of fire and creativity, and Lakshmi, representing earth and material manifestations, offer Anne two role models to identify with.

Though I sensed Anne's disappointment with the limitation of her love relationship, I felt this card spread was encouraging her to focus her creativity upon developing a new business under consideration. Besides fulfilling her artistic desires, this would take some of the pressure off her love relationship so it could develop naturally.

Card 1: The card representing the overview of Anne's situation is the King of Swords. This powerful card, related to the goddess Isis, symbolized to me Anne's desire to control and define the love relationship for herself rather than through its limitations. I also felt that this card was an invitation for her to embody more of the masculine, business-oriented energy of the King of Swords.

Card 2: Again, swords show up as a force to be considered. The Seven of Swords shows that she is wondering if she needs to gather her swords in order to protect herself against disappointment. It also suggests a pulling away from her loved one to consider the situation and the dangers inherent in it.

Card 3: The major arcana card Contemplation, related to the goddess Chang O, suggests that Anne has been spending a lot of time alone thinking. This card, related to the moon (Chang O is a Chinese lunar goddess), also shows that her emotions are running high. She needs to withdraw to consider them. Since this was the only Major Arcana card in this spread, it is at the heart of her reading.

Card 4: Interestingly enough, another king is positioned in her past. This time he is the King of Staves, showing that Anne is full of creative inspiration which could be successfully implemented. When I asked her about this, she admitted she was considering starting a new business, one that would emphasize her creative talents more than her current job does.

Card 5: More staves—this time, the Ten of Staves. At this time Anne wants resolution; she feels overwhelmed by responsibility for the relationship and doesn't know how much more she can take.

Card 6: In Anne's near future, the Four of Pentacles signifies the solidity she can create with her business as well as the wealth she can manifest. It also suggests that her love relationship will be on more solid footing — remember, pentacles (especially fours) symbolize the manifestation of desires on the material level.

Card 7: The Three of Pentacles shows how Anne is able to focus her energies into constructive action rather than getting swept up in emotional highs and lows.

Card 8: Others admire Anne's talents. They see her as the Princess of Pentacles, able to create wonderful practical things that enrich people's lives as well as herself.

Card 9: Deep in her heart, Anne knows that to be happy she needs to embody the creative energy of the Queen of Staves; she enjoys being busy and inspired.

Card 10: Despite the Venusian flavor of Anne's query, the only cup card she chose for this reading was the Five of Cups (remember, cups are affiliated with the goddess Venus). Yes, she is disappointed with her relationship at this time. But she also needs to focus upon the positive in her love relationship rather than the negative. She must decide what is right for her and, if necessary, move on to a more satisfying relationship.

When I had finished Anne's reading, she chose a final card for additional clarity. I was not surprised to see that it was the Eight of Pentacles, the card of the craftwoman. This seemed to reiterate the overall message of her reading: time to work!

Sample Reading #4:
The Relationship Cross

Sabrina, a 42 year-old writer, had a fight with her brother that ended with him swearing never to speak with her again. Shaken but resolute that she was in the right, she asked for a tarot reading to clarify the situation. The Relationship Cross spread seemed an ideal choice for examining the issues involved.

As we went over the cards together, I felt that this rupture was not permanent and that there were deeper issues at play. In addition, the presence of cards from all four minor arcana suits and the major arcana suggested that many forces were at work here. Sabrina admitted that her brother had a substance abuse problem; while it was not serious enough to keep him from functioning in the world, it did affect him in other ways. He also had a tendency to rely upon others for financial help, as well as a need to blame others for his personal discontents. But Sabrina was perhaps trying too hard to make him see the self-destructive quality of his life; any attempts she made to help were rebuffed, which made her feel negated.

As mentioned earlier in this section, the Relationship Cross is read in an unusual manner, taking into consideration four groups of three cards, each representing a different area of the question.

Cards 11 through 13: Although occasionally she must juggle her finances (indicated by the Two and Three of Pentacles), Sabrina has been able to construct her life in such a way that she is very self-sufficient. She feels pride in her accomplishments; it is difficult for freelancers to make a living and she is able to do so. This speaks to her disappointment in her brother's lack of self-

8 Six of Swords						
9 Four of Staves						
10 XVI Oppression						

| 1
Nine
of Cups | 2
XIII
Transfor-
mation | 3
XXI
The World | 4
Four of
Pentacles | 5
King of
Pentacles | 6
Seven of
Cups | 7
Four of
Cups |

| 11
Two of
Pentacles |
| 12
XIX
The Sun |
| 13
Three of
Pentacles |

Sample Reading #4:
The Relationship Cross Spread

sufficiency; she is unable to understand why he doesn't share her values of hard work and independence. The Sun, a Major Arcana card related to the Zorya, a trinity of Slavic solar goddesses, also sounds a life issue for her: as a writer, Sabrina has a mission to use words to bring light into the world. Hence, it bothers her greatly that her words do not influence her brother as easily as they do others.

Cards 1 through 3: More major arcana cards depict the extreme changes Sabrina is experiencing at this time. Sabrina chose Transformation, The World (in an upside-down, or reversed, position), and the Nine of Cups to represent herself right now. She feels a sense of blessedness about her life's journey. But she also feels like something is holding her back; her brother personifies this blockage for her. She is also frightened because she feels their relationship is dying; she wishes instead for closure and transformation. The World (affiliated with the goddess Gaia) in a reversed position shows that Sabrina feels their fight mirrors what is preventing her from moving out into the world in a literal sense.

Cards 5 through 7: The Seven of Cups in a reversed position shows that Sabrina's brother is caught up in negative fantasies and unable to act. He is also in a state of denial about the effects of his actions. But the Four of Cups shows that on some level he does want to shake things up; he is using Sabrina as a catalyst. A preponderance of cups in weakened positions suggests that he may be drowning in the shadow side of Venus: decadence, fantasy, emotionalism for the sake of display. The King of Pentacles shows he is relying on others to bail him out financially; what he really needs now is the structure this king represents.

Cards 8 through 10: In the future, Sabrina will understand her brother's limitations (Six of Swords); she will also realize that she cannot help him unless he wants help. This will allow her to move on to a new phase of life where she won't feel so influenced by his problems. The Four of Staves also shows that she is creating her own home and setting boundaries; but the major arcana card Oppression suggests there still is work to do before their relationship can be comfortable again.

Card 4: For the outcome, the Prince of Staves invites Sabrina to focus on the movement in her own life. She needs to personify the powerful energy of Freyja, the Norse goddess of creativity and beauty. Since Freyja also has aspects as a war goddess, this card also suggests that Sabrina needs to be prepared for further combat; most likely she and her brother will fight again. While it is possible that a warm dialogue can be created out of conflict, it may be a while before there is any resolution—but hopefully, Sabrina now understands the situation enough not to expect anything else.

FURTHER READINGS

Like any tool, mastering the tarot is a journey that takes time, study, and thought; hopefully, *The Goddess Tarot* will whet your interest to continue learning about the tarot and goddesses. What follows is a list of several books that I felt a philosophical agreement with, or were particularly helpful to me, during the years of my involvement with the tarot and while creating *The Goddess Tarot*. So many wonderful books are available about the tarot that it is impossible to list them all; perhaps these can serve as an introduction:

Gearhart, Sally and Susan Rennie. *A Feminist Tarot*.
    Alyson Publications, 1997.

Greer, Mary K. *Tarot for Your Self; A Workbook for Personal
    Transformation*. Newcastle Publishing Co., Inc., 1984.

Palmer, Helen (introduction), Signe E. Echols, M. S., Robert Mueller, Ph.D.,
    and Sandra A. Thomson. *Spiritual Tarot: Seventy-Eight Paths
    to Personal Development*. Avon Books, New York, 1996.

Shavick, Nancy. *The Tarot*. Berkley Publishing Group, 1988.

Stuart, Micheline. *The Tarot Path to Self-Development*.
    Shambhala Publications, 1996.

For those of you who would like to learn more about goddesses, the following books are invaluable to any student of feminist mythology or spirituality. More extensive bibliographies can also be found in my books *The Book of Goddesses* and *Embracing the Goddess Within: A Creative Guide for Women:*

Ann, Martha, and Dorothy Myers Imel. *Goddesses in World Mythology.*
    Oxford University Press, 1993.

Baring, Anne, and Jules Cashford. *The Myth of the Goddess.*
    Viking Books, 1992.

Grimal, Pierre, editor. *Larousse World Mythology.*
    Hamlyn Publishing Group, 1968.

Larrington, Carolyne, editor. *The Feminist Companion to Mythology.*
    Pandora/Harper Collins, 1992.

Monaghan, Patricia. *The Book of Goddesses and Heroines.*
    Llewellyn Publications, 1993.

Stone, Merlin. *When God Was a Woman.*
    Harvest/Harcourt Brace Jovanovich Books, 1976.

Walker, Barbara C. *The Woman's Encyclopedia of Myths and Secrets.*
    Harper San Francisco, 1983.

ॐ ॐ ॐ

I hope this deck and book will bring the beauty and wisdom of the Divine Feminine into your life. As you work with *The Goddess Tarot,* I'd love to hear any experiences or thoughts you may have— please feel free to contact me via www.artandwords.com. You can also visit the Goddess Tarot website at www.goddesstarot.com.

And thank you for supporting my work!